THE EASY WAY
TO BETTER GRADES

THE EASY WAY TO BETTER GRADES

REVISED EDITION

by

OTIS D. FROE, Ph.D.

Director of Research and Evaluation,
Morgan State College

and

OTYCE B. FROE, M. A.

Baltimore City Public Schools

ARCO PUBLISHING COMPANY, INC.

219 Park Avenue South, New York, N.Y. 10003

Published by ARCO PUBLISHING COMPANY, Inc.
219 Park Avenue South, New York, N.Y. 10003

Second Edition, Second Printing, 1978

Formerly titled: How To Become A Successful Student

Library of Congress Catalog Card Number: 73-76959
Paper Edition: ISBN: 0-668-03352-5
Cloth Edition: ISBN: 0-668-03353-3

Printed in the United States of America

Table of Contents

Preface

It is widely believed that somehow students automatically acquire study skills, habits and attitudes that are essential for success in school work. This belief is not founded in fact. Students acquire study and learning skills by application of knowledge and conscious effort, just as they acquire other kinds of skills.

The basic purpose of this book is to help the student to develop the kinds of skills he needs to succeed in school work. This book is not theoretical. It is a *practical guide* in methods of study and learning. It was developed through practical experiences in helping students learn how to study, to read and listen effectively, to take notes, quizzes and examinations, and to make effective use of educational resources and facilities. It is assumed that the student who uses this book actually *wants* to master the art of studying effectively. This book, therefore, does not attempt to persuade the student that he should devote time and effort to improve himself, but seeks to provide him with the tools by which he can effectively use his potential for learning. However, the student who approaches the materials in this book in a serious manner will, no doubt, *see the need to devote time and serious effort* to improving his learning potential.

This book is written for all students, whether studying full- or part-time. It is intended for use at the high school level, in college freshmen orientation programs, in remedial and "how to study" courses, in courses designed to prepare high school students for college work, and in adult-education groups. Also, it is intended as a self-help guide for the student who seeks through his own initiative to develop skills for undertaking serious study and learning. It should also prove especially helpful for high school students applying for *advanced placement* in college. Many students will find college work more demanding than high school study and will have a greater need for more effective "tools" and techniques for doing college work.

O. D. F.
O. B. F.

To the Student

The need for this book, How To BECOME A SUCCESSFUL STUDENT, is due to the fact that far too many students are *not* successful. At one time it was assumed that students fail in school work mainly because they lack scholastic ability or intelligence. However, we recognize now that students fail most often because they do not know how to study efficiently. The number of students who do not succeed is startling. It is estimated that out of every one hundred freshmen throughout the country who enter college, only thirty-nine remain to graduate. Approximately 11 percent of these freshmen drop out by the end of the *first semester,* and 28 percent by the end of the *freshman year.* A similar situation exists in the high schools where it is reported that forty out of every one hundred students who enter high school drop out before graduating. A large percentage of these drop-outs would not occur if students knew how to study efficiently.

Three factors are necessary for success in school work. They are *ability,* sometimes referred to as scholastic aptitude or intelligence; *interest in school work,* which usually results from a clear understanding of aims and goals; and *efficient methods of study.* Insofar as ability is concerned, it has become customary to expect only students who make high scores on so-called tests of intelligence to succeed in school or college. This is no longer true, except perhaps in some private schools which select students on the basis of their high ranking on intelligence or aptitude tests. In most public or state supported schools there is a wide range of abilities among students, and many students of so-called "average" ability succeed notably. In fact, a study made of students enrolled in universities revealed that the type of individual encountered most often is the student of *average* ability, who is socially well-adjusted, but is quite unsettled in his orientation to life. The skills, *abilities* and understandings needed to do school work are largely *developed* over

9

the years. They are not, as many imply, fixed by heredity. These abilities can be, and are, changed as a result of exposures to environments favorable to learning—in school and out.

The factor of interest is highly important and is directly related to success in school. It is the thing that keeps you pushing on toward your goal when the "going gets tough." Usually interest is present when you have a goal and work persistently toward it. Like "school ability," we are not born with a definite set of interests. Interests are likewise developed as we live and come into contact with our many environments.

The third factor, efficient methods of study, is, perhaps most important to school success. The realization of the importance of this factor is the reason for this book. The purpose of the book is to help you get firmly within your grasp the "know how" for successful study and learning. The aim is to help you acquire attitudes and skills that will result in a high level of study and learning efficiency. This "know how" in study will enable you to complete learning tasks with a minimum of time and effort. You will not only experience increased learning from your efforts, but will find that you are able to retain more of what you do learn, and for a longer period of time. The materials presented in this book have not been "dreamed up" by the writers, but are based on sound principles of learning. They have been tried out with many students and have been found to produce desired results. This book is not written primarily for the student experiencing difficulty in school work or for the average and below average student. It is for *all* students. Students of all levels of ability can profit from its use. The book offers no magical formula or easy way by which you can acquire the attitudes and skills necessary for effective study and learning. Nothing that it offers can take the place of a sound determination on your part to *increase* your study and learning efficiency. You must decide for yourself, first of all, that you *want* to learn to study.

Learning requires the formation of new habits of thinking and acting. In this connection, you must bear in mind that you probably have some inefficient habits and attitudes which you did not acquire overnight nor will you be able to replace these habits with more constructive ones overnight. Habit formation and *change* in existing habits require *time* and *persistent effort*. This book will help to identify ineffective study habits and attitudes, and will suggest ways of formulating constructive ones to take their place. The fact that you own this book is not enough. You must use it faithfully and intensively. Give yourself a fair chance. Do not skip a single page. Do all the exercises and problems. These are included to make the materials more meaningful to you. Begin immediately to apply the principles and techniques you learn from this book to your school work. Specifically, this book will help you do the following:

Build attitudes and habits necessary for effective study and learning

Look at life goals and learning situations in proper perspective.

Set up an effective study environment

Select and arrange study facilities to increase concentration and learning.

Plan a study schedule

Make the maximum use of time through wise planning of activities.

Acquire basic techniques of study

Formulate habits that will result in increased learning and retention.

Acquire skill in note-taking

Increase learning and retention through the proper recording of important ideas gained from reading or listening.

Acquire skill in using library facilities

Increase learning through the use of books and related materials.

Acquire effective reading skills

Develop an adequate vocabulary, increase reading rate and level of comprehension.

Improving writing skills.

Writing a class report or term paper.

Acquire effective listening skills

Apprehend the speaker's purpose, grasp and organize his ideas.

Develop skill in taking examinations and quizzes

Perform better on examinations as a result of an increased "know-how" in taking tests.

Learn how to do assignments

Acquire a basic procedure in attacking all school assignments.

Develop and maintain top learning efficiency

Acquire mental and physical health habits that will result in increased personal efficiency.

Test your present knowledge about some of the important principles related to study and learning. Take the quiz which appears in Exercise I. After you have answered *every* item according to the directions given, determine your score (the number of correct answers) by consulting the key which appears in the appendix. Make a note of your score. When you have finished your study of this book, take this quiz again and compare your two performances on the quiz. Do not consult the key until you have marked each item with a plus (+) or minus (—).

EXERCISE I

Pre-Test: Principles of Study and Learning

Drections: In the parenthesis ( ) before each statement place a plus (+) if the statement is true; place a minus (—) if the statement is false.

( ) 1. You should spend about four hours per week in studying for a class which meets one hour each day for three days a week.

( ) 2. Listening to soft music while studying helps you to concentrate.

( ) 3. The place *where* you study or the time *when* you study has little effect on your power of concentration.

( ) 4. If you study with a room-mate the best position for the two desks is side by side.

( ) 5. The most desirable temperature for study, for most persons, is around 68° F.

( ) 6. In order to prevent glare from artificial light when study-ing, the only light in the room should be that on the study table or desk.

( ) 7. Your ability to concentrate will be increased if you will relax on a couch while studying.

( ) 8. Highly intelligent persons are able to give *full* and *complete attention* to several things at the same time.

( ) 9. If your ability to concentrate is good, it is all right to study and engage in conversation at the same time.

( ) 10. Eating a large meal just before studying stimulates you to learn effectively.

( ) 11. You should refrain from activity of any kind for several minutes after you sit down at your desk for study.

( ) 12. The average student in college will be able to pursue a normal class load of 15 to 17 semester hours if his outside job requires him to work no more than six hours per day.

( ) 13. It is a good policy to keep notes for all your classes in one notebook.

( ) 14. A study session for difficult subjects should last without a break for about four hours.

( ) 15. In subjects of average difficulty, it is better to study for three hours at a time than to divide the study period into two periods lasting 1½ hours each with a rest period in between.

( ) 16. Chemistry, physics, mathematics, Spanish, French, and sociology are best studied in that order than the follow-ing order: chemistry, Spanish, mathematics, sociology, physics, French.

( ) 17. It is a good policy to revise your class notes for each sub-ject at the end of each *week*.

( ) 18. For the average student, a review once every two weeks in each subject is sufficient.

( ) 19. If you have a good memory, preparing for an examina-tion by "cramming" is just as effective as preparation by regular study and review.

( ) 20. A good rule to observe while taking examinations is to "work as rapidly as you can, but as carefully as you can."

( ) 21. It requires years of retraining to become an efficient reader if you have bad reading habits at the present time.

( ) 22. Rapid readers have as good an understanding of what they read as do slow, cautious readers.

( ) 23. Speed in reading is unimportant so long as one understands what he reads.

( ) 24. When taking an examination, you should spend more time in thinking about the answer than in writing it.

( ) 25. If notes taken in class are to be useful, they should be in the form of complete sentences rather than in short phrases and abbreviations.

( ) 26. To locate a book in the library, you must know both the author's name and the title of the book.

( ) 27. If a person can read well, it follows that he can listen effectively also.

( ) 28. The average person spends more time in listening than in writing, speaking, or reading.

( ) 29. The index of the encyclopedia is the best source to consult in locating all of the important information about a subject in the encyclopedia.

( ) 30. Before you can locate the title of a book in the library card catalogue, you must first know the name of the author.

Building Attitudes and Habits for Study and Learning

Attitudes and habits play an important part in acquiring the kinds of study skills that will result in maximum learning. The process of acquiring any skill involves the breaking of old habits or ways of acting and replacing them with more constructive habits. Basic to the changing of habits is the factor of attitude. One must first determine that he wants to change a habit. The most important step in building effective study skills is the acquiring of an attitude or a *genuine desire and determination* to change from ineffective methods of study to effective ones. One essential in the acquiring of wholesome study and learning attitudes is the ability to see your life goals and study and learning situations in proper perspective. That is, you must be able to see a *real* relationship between what you want to *do* or *be* and the many hours you spend in study and learning. In order to see this relationship, you must first be *aware* of the goals toward which you are working. The more clearly you are able to recognize your goals, the more obvious will be this relationship. Are your goals clear to you at this moment? Ask yourself this question: What will I be doing five years from now? Ten years from now? Twenty years? If you cannot satisfactorily answer this question, or if your answer is characterized by uncertainty, stop now and give some serious thought to the question of your life's work. The matter of clear goals pertains to other phases of living as well as to occupational goals. It is equally important to ask yourself the question: What kind of a person do I want to *be* five years from now? Ten years from now? Twenty years? Do you have in mind the kind of social or cultural skills you would like to attain? School counselors, teachers, and parents are able to give you valuable assistance in the process of thinking through your life goals. They can help you to look objectively at your aspirations or goals in terms of your abilities and interests, and to help you plan a course of action to reach these goals if they are reasonable. They can also help you to select other goals if the ones you have selected are not in keeping with your abilities and interests.

Once you have a clear picture of the direction in which you are heading, and the possible ways of reaching your goals, study and learning situations tend to become meaningful to you. School subjects, for example, will mean more than stumbling blocks between you and a high school diploma, or a college degree. Your studies will come to mean a way of acquiring *needed skills* rather than a procedure for acquiring grades. Assume, for example, that you aspire to be a certified public accountant, and that this is for you a reasonable goal. If you have a very vivid picture of this goal, you may even see yourself as director of *your own* accounting firm. Then begin to visualize the specific duties you will have to perform—the kinds of skills you will need to have. If you have some familiarity with accounting you will know, for example, that in this occupation you will need to be skillful in working with numbers, bookkeeping, examining financial statements, preparing financial statements, conducting financial investigations, computing taxes, etc. When once you see yourself performing these duties, the study of mathematics, economics, business administration, finance takes on a definite meaning. You begin to study mathematics not for the teacher, but to acquire skills you will need in your life's work. Examine *your* occupational goal in this manner. If you are not familiar with the specific skills that are required in your selected occupation, talk with your school counselor, read books on the occupation, or better still, talk with someone who is now working at the same occupation. A good source to consult is the *Dictionary of Occupational Titles* found in many libraries. This dictionary describes in detail duties performed in many different kinds of occupations.

You can look at cultural goals in the same manner as you examine your occupational goals. Ask yourself what kind of a person do you want to *be* five years from now? Ten years from now? Twenty years? What kind of things do you want to be able to do? What kind of skills do you want to possess? For example, if you see yourself as a person who is skillful in the use of the English Language, then the importance of an adequate vocabulary becomes meaningful to you. You will want to learn new words not for the teacher, but in order to be able to express your thoughts clearly both in speaking and writing. You will see the study of Latin, for example, as a means of increasing your English vocabulary. You will less likely be bored by Latin as are many students who see it only as a study of a "dead" language with no practical use.

A clarity of purpose or goals, then, will assist you in formulating wholesome attitudes relating to study and learning. After acquiring the proper attitudes, the next step is to formulate the habits necessary for effective study and learning. After you have made a determination that you want to improve your study and learning skills, study the principles below relating to habit formation. Apply these principles when attempting to acquire the basic study skills discussed in the following sections of this book.

Launch into the new habit with full force and vigor.

Tell your friends of your new plans. Make it difficult to revert to your old ways without "losing face." Avoid situations which will cause you to back down on your new resolution. If, for example, you resolve to form the habit of studying in the same place each day and know that your friends usually drop by your room for leisure conversation, then don't select this room as the place to begin the formation of the habit. Select another room, inform your friends that you will not be available for conversation, or do whatever else is practical in helping you to avoid the temptation to put off the beginning of the habit. This practice is very important, especially in the **early stages** of your habit formation. Another good rule is to **impose** penalties on yourself. Do everything that is *not* in keeping with the old habit you are trying to break. For example, you resolve to set aside one hour each week for a review in each of your school subjects. Don't make any engagements which will interfere wth these review periods. Leave off the special party which has been planned by the gang if it comes during one of these review periods.

Never permit an exception until the new habit is established.

Don't skip one of your review periods, for example, by telling yourself that you will review twice as long the coming week. If you resolve to begin study promptly at 8:00 p.m. each day, don't permit yourself to put it off until 8:30 p.m.—begin sharply at 8:00 p.m. even if you have to forego some other activity. This is especially important where some previous unplanned activity will run over into a planned activity. Go promptly to your place of study at the planned time even if your mind is still on the previous activity. Go through the motions of study. *Concentration will come.* Each lapse into an old habit or each exception made lessens the chance of the new habit becoming established.

Find an opportunity to act on a new resolution at once.

For example, if you resolve to revise and study your chemistry notes each day immediately after the chemistry lecture or demonstration, begin this practice the *first* day you attend the lecture or demonstration. Don't tell yourself that you will begin next week. Waiting until next week will destroy enthusiasm which is necessary in habit formation. Take the first step while you are still "worked up" about the idea.

Assume an active attitude when forming a new habit.

If, for example, you decide to begin the writing of a theme on a certain day and find that when the time comes you just aren't "in the mood" to begin this work, don't permit yourself to put it off till later. Sit down at your place of study as planned. Begin *immediately* to go through the acts of preparation for writing the theme. Fill your pen, open your books, get out your notes, start to write. The point is *do something* related to your assignment. Concentration will come if you go through the motions of study. Almost before you know it you are studying. Don't permit yourself to postpone study or to "fool around" once you sit down to study.

The foregoing principles are basic to habit formation. Observe them carefully when attempting to formulate new habits of study. Also remember that attitudes greatly influence your behavior—the way you choose to do things. Some attitudes are advantageous; others handicap you. Desirable attitudes *can* be acquired, and effective study habits *can* be formed if you have determined that you want to do something about your present attitudes and habits. You must make this determination if you are to develop the kinds of skills that will result in a high level of learning efficiency.

EXERCISE II

A. If you have made a decision as to your life's work (at least a tentative decision), list this occupation. Also list the basic skills you will need to acquire if you are to be successful with this work. If you are not aware of the skills needed for this work, consult your counselor or your teachers to obtain information concerning the sources you might use in obtaining more information about your chosen occupation.

B. Make a list of the *social skills* needed by an adult if he is to be an effective citizen in our culture.

C. If you have not made at least a tentative decision about your life's work, make several appointments to talk with a counselor or teacher about your life-work plans.

STUDY ENVIRONMENT

POOR STUDENT

GOOD STUDENT

SECTION II

Arranging The Study Environment

It is important that you set up what is for you a good study environment. The elements making for an effective study place will not be the same for all persons. You will have to find out what works for you. Many successful students, however, have found the following principles, relating to study environment, to be very helpful.

SELECTING A ROOM FOR STUDY

Select a room that will be available each day, and if possible, at the same time each day.

Using the same place for study makes possible a "mind-set" necessary for concentration.

If possible, select a room in which the study desk will not have to be shared.

Select a room where it will be possible to "leave things out" after you have finished a period of study. This is not possible if someone else will need to use the same study desk or table. Much valuable time is lost if you have to put study materials away and then re-assemble them each time you sit down to study. If you have a room where your study equipment will not be disturbed, or where you do not have to clean up for the next person using the room, you will be able to launch directly into your study without all the preliminary preparation of "setting things up" for study. Much of your enthusiasm can be lost in such preliminary preparation.

Select a room where traffic or other distractions are at a minimum.

Select a room where the door can be closed if there is apt to be much traffic by the room. It may be necessary to hang a

"Do not disturb" sign outside your door until your family or friends get accustomed to the idea that you are not to be disturbed while studying.

Provide for good air circulation in the room.

Cross circulation of air is desirable. A room lacking sufficient oxygen tends to reduce both mental and physical efficiency. Concentration demands that both your mental and physical efficiency be at a maximum. A relative humidity of 50% is also desirable.

Maintain a moderate room temperature.

A room temperature below 70° F (perhaps around 68° F) for most persons is best for effective study and learning. A moderate temperature encourages *activity* and *alertness*. The most comfortable relative humidity is from 40 to 60 percent.

Provide for adequate lighting in the room.

Average study conditions require 25 to 30 candles (candlefoot as a unit of light measurement) on the desk. In addition to light supplied by the desk or table lamp, the entire room should be adequately lighted. This additional room light prevents undesirable contrast which comes from having study desk or table lighted while the surroundings are dark. Contrast is conducive to eye strain and hastens fatigue. The lighting of the entire room is best accomplished by the use of overhead lamps equipped with shields which reflect a part of the light upward, and transmit a part of it downward in a diffused state. Fluorescent lamps equipped with louvers provide a desirable type of lighting for the room.

SELECTING AND ARRANGING THE DESK FOR STUDY

Select a study desk that is conducive to good posture.

Your desk should be of a size or height to allow comfortable upright posture with your feet touching the floor.

Select a study desk with sufficient top surface.

The top of the study desk should be of sufficient size so as to permit you to spread out all the equipment and materials you may need for a particular assignment. Being cramped for space may lead to confusion and frustration. Also, all equipment and materials to be used in an assignment should be within easy reach either on the desk top, or in a drawer or compartment. Having to get up from the desk to get equipment or materials interferes with concentration.

Select a study desk that does not have a highly polished working surface.

If the desk has a highly polished surface, cover it with a blotter or find some other means to tone down the finish. Glare tends to cause eye strain and produces early fatigue. A common household remedy for toning down glaring finishes on furniture (table and desk tops) is to rub the surface with a cloth dipped in buttermilk, and then polish the surface with a dry cloth. The acid in the milk is sufficient to tone down the glare but will not cause damage to the finish of the surface.

Arrange the study desk so as to reduce distractions.

Do not place the desk near a window unless the window is equipped with suitable blinds which will shut out distractions but not daylight. Venetian type blinds serve this purpose. Also, if you have a roommate arrange the desk so that you have your backs to each other while studying.

Keep the desk top free from distracting materials.

Keep everything off the desk that is not to be used in study. This includes pictures, ornaments, mementos, etc. These lessen your ability to concentrate.

Select a study desk with sufficient storage space.

The desk should have storage space for the *basic* materials to be used in all of your study. These materials will include a good dictionary, general reference books, paper, ink, erasers, paper clips, blotters, transparent tape, ruler, compass, protractor, etc.

EXERCISE III

A. Make a list of all the things you find wrong with your present study environment.

B. List the *specific* things you plan to do to improve this study environment. Work to accomplish each improvement, if only one at a time. As each improvement is made, cross it off your list.

SECTION III

Planning a Schedule

After you have arranged the best possible environment for study, the next step is to develop a *specific plan* for study—a plan that is definite, but at the same time flexible enough so that you actually will be able to follow it. Unsuccessful students make the mistake of allowing their school work to pile up because they have neglected to make any definite plan for study. You will find that there is enough time for your study and other activities if you follow a schedule that has been planned to enable you to make the maximum use of your time. You will not only be able to find enough time for your other activities, but you will also accomplish more in the way of study and learning. A definite plan for study increases concentration. If you establish the habit of studying a subject at the same time each day, you will find that less effort is required in focusing your attention on it. By planning and following a a study schedule, you avoid the last minute cram-sessions before a quiz or examination. Cramming is a risky type of learning. Not only are materials learned through cram-sessions quickly forgotten, but cramming is likely to bring on emotional disturbances which will greatly impair your mental efficiency at a time when you need to be mentally alert.

The following basic principles concerning schedule making should be studied thoroughly before you attempt to formulate a plan for study.

Make a flexible schedule.

Your schedule should be such that it can be adjusted to meet unexpected events. If it becomes imperative that you use a period previously scheduled for study for something you did not expect, you should be able to "trade" this period for

Time	Monday	Tuesday	Wednes-day	Thursday	Friday	Saturday	Sunday
6-7	←――――――――――――――― Dress ――――――――――――――――→						↑
7-8	←――――――――――― Break-fast ―――――――――――→						
8-9	French 102	Study History	French 102	Study History	French 102	↑	
9-10	English 101	Study History	English 101	Study History	English 101		
10-11	Study French		Study French		Study French	Personal Activities, Part-Time Job, Special Study and Review, Etc.	Church and Other Personal Activities – Special Study and Reviews
11-12	Study French	Physical Ed. 190	Study French	Physical Ed. 190	Study French		
12-1	←――――――――――――――― Lunch ――――――――――――――→						
1-2	Math. 114	Math. 114	Math. 114	Math. 114	Review English		
2-3	History 101	Study Phy. Ed.	History 101	Study Phy. Ed.	History 101		
3-4	Study English	Study History	Study English	―――	Study English		
4-5	Study English	Study History	Study English	Review Math.	Study English		
5-6	←――――――――――――――― Dinner ―――――――――――――→						
6-7	←――――――――――――――― Dinner ―――――――――――――→						
7-8	Study Math.	Study Math.	Study Math.	Study Math.	Review French		
8-9	Study Math.	Study Math.	Study Math.	Study Math.	Review History		
9-10	Free Time: Reading, recreation special study, sleep etc.						
10-11	" "	"	"	" "	" "		
11-12	" "	"	"	" "	" "	↓	↓
Total Study Hours = 32	6	7	6	6	7	Weekly Total Class Hrs. = 15	

NOTE: Physical Education 190 is a course in swimming. Only two hours of study per week have been scheduled. Review periods are interchangeable.

Fig. 1. A Typical College Study Schedule: 15 hours of class work and 32 hours of study

SCHEDULE
STUDY - RECREATION - WORK - REST

Time	Monday	Tuesday	Wednesday	Thursday	Friday	Saturday	Sunday
6-7 a.m.							
7-8 a.m.							
8-9 a.m.							
9-10 a.m.							
10-11 a.m.							
11-12 N							
12-1 p.m.							
1-2 p.m.							
2-3 p.m.							
3-4 p.m.							
4-5 p.m.							
5-6 p.m.							
6-7 p.m.							
7-8 p.m.							
8-9 p.m.							
9-10 p.m.							
10-11 p.m.							
11-12 M							
Total Class Hours→							
Total Study Hours→							

SCHEDULE
STUDY - RECREATION - WORK - REST

Time	Monday	Tuesday	Wednes-day	Thursday	Friday	Saturday	Sunday
6-7 a.m.							
7-8 a.m.							
8-9 a.m.							
9-10 a.m.							
10-11 a.m.							
11-12 N							
12-1 p.m.							
1-2 p.m.							
2-3 p.m.							
3-4 p.m.							
4-5 p.m.							
5-6 p.m.							
6-7 p.m.							
7-8 p.m.							
8-9 p.m.							
9-10 p.m.							
10-11 p.m.							
11-12 M							
Total Class Hours→							
Total Study Hours→							

SCHEDULE
STUDY - RECREATION - WORK - REST

Time	Monday	Tuesday	Wednesday	Thursday	Friday	Saturday	Sunday
6-7 a.m.							
7-8 a.m.							
8-9 a.m.							
9-10 a.m.							
10-11 a.m.							
11-12 N							
12-1 p.m.							
1-2 p.m.							
2-3 p.m.							
3-4 p.m.							
4-5 p.m.							
5-6 p.m.							
6-7 p.m.							
7-8 p.m.							
8-9 p.m.							
9-10 p.m.							
10-11 p.m.							
11-12 M							
Total Class Hours→							
Total Study Hours→							

SCHEDULE
STUDY - RECREATION - WORK - REST

Time	Monday	Tuesday	Wednes-day	Thursday	Friday	Saturday	Sunday
6-7 a.m.							
7-8 a.m.							
8-9 a.m.							
9-10 a.m.							
10-11 a.m.							
11-12 N							
12-1 p.m.							
1-2 p.m.							
2-3 p.m.							
3-4 p.m.							
4-5 p.m.							
5-6 p.m.							
6-7 p.m.							
7-8 p.m.							
8-9 p.m.							
9-10 p.m.							
10-11 p.m.							
11-12 M							
Total Class Hours→							
Total Study Hours→							

another period. You should have free periods on the schedule which may be used for a lost study period. This trading of periods might mean that you have to sacrifice a part of your recreation time. However, it is more important to *trade* time for study rather than lose it.

Plan enough time for study.

The number of hours set aside for study on your schedule should be at least twice the number of hours you spend in class each week. A general rule is that for every class hour in each subject, you should plan 2 hours of study. You will perhaps need to have additional study periods available just before examinations or for special assignments. Some subjects may be difficult for you and require more than 2 hours. Other subjects may not require as much time. Physical education activities courses might come in this category.

Arrange your schedule to fit your personality.

Plan to study a subject at a time when you can give it your greatest energy. If, for example, you find that the study of German is difficult for you, and you can do your best work early in the morning, then schedule the study of German for the morning hours. Since it has been found that you forget less when study is followed by sleep, you might arrange to study certain of your difficult subjects just before retiring, but while you are still alert and wide awake.

Plan for weekly reviews.

Include in your schedule *at least* one hour each week for a review in each of your subjects. You may need to schedule additional review periods just before a quiz or an examination.

Make use of free periods during the school day.

Plan to use most of the free time between 8:00 a.m. and 4:00 p.m. for study. This includes the free time between classes or other school activities. This time is likely to be lost unless you definitely plan in your schedule to use it.

Plan a study period to follow the class period.

Where possible, schedule study periods for a particular subject immediately following the class for that subject. If the period cannot be scheduled immediately to follow the class, then attempt to schedule the period for study immediately preceding the class. The practice of scheduling study immediately after class is very important when the assignment is closely related to a lecture or class discussion. You have a chance to attack the assignment while the materials are still "fresh."

Plan study periods so that rest or dissimilar activities come between closely related learning activities.

So arrange your periods of study that you follow the study of one subject with a subject which is as much unlike the first subject as possible. For example, if you plan to study abnormal psychology, social psychology, and chemistry during one evening, it is better to plan your schedule so as to study social psychology, chemistry, and then abnormal psychology than to study the two psychologies in succession. The study of 2 subjects in succession which have similar content or involve similar skills tends to be followed by a higher rate of forgetting than would be the case if the two subjects were dissimilar. If the study of a subject cannot be followed by the study of a dissimilar subject, then a rest period should come immediately after the first study period.

Space your study periods.

Plan your schedule so that not more than 1½ or 2 hours are spent in the study of any subject at one sitting. After a moderate period of intensive study, introduce a rest period or a change in activity. If you can't use the study break for rest, then study an entirely different subject. However, for greater learning returns, a period of rest or relaxation is more desirable than a change in activity. Prolonged mental activity without sufficient rest periods results in lowered learning efficiency.

When you have studied the above principles carefully, examine the sample schedule and begin to plan your own schedule. (Fig. 1) You may begin your schedule by writing in all of the activities you have to perform at a fixed time. These will include your class and laboratory periods, time for eating, your job, sleeping, etc. It is a good practice to make the first draft of your schedule with a pencil. This will enable you to make changes. It is also a good practice to enter fixed classes with a red pencil. Also indicate the exact time you will study each subject, and also the time you plan to review each subject each week. Indicate your recreational activities on your schedule. After you have finished a rough draft of your schedule, check it against the basic principles presented to see if they have been observed in your schedule. It is especially important that you count the hours you have allowed for study to see if you have provided at least two hours of study for each class hour in each subject. After you have checked your schedule, let your counselor or teacher examine it. If no further changes are recommended, then copy it in final form. You may want to make more than one copy. Perhaps one for your notebook, and one to be placed on or near your study desk.

EXERCISE IV

Using Fig. 1 as a model, and by following the principles discussed in this section, construct a study schedule for your present school classes. Use one of the study schedule forms provided for making a rough draft of this schedule. After you have discussed this first draft with a counselor or teacher, and all of the necessary corrections have been made, copy this schedule on one of the other forms. It is a good idea to make two copies—one to be kept with you in your notebook, and the other to be kept near your study desk at home.

Developing Study and Learning Techniques

The following suggestions concerning study procedures are based on a careful analysis of the habits of students who are successful with school work, and on current theories of learning. The procedures suggested are basic to *all* study and learning situations. Use them in formulating your own study procedures.

Do all of your studying in the same place. (In your own room if possible)

Familiarity with one study room will mean fewer distractions and greater concentration. The furnishings in a room which you see over and over again soon lose their power to distract you. You get to the place where you "see them but do not see them." Also, when you use the same room each day, you establish a mindset in which you come to associate the room with study and concentration. As mentioned earlier, the use of your own room makes it unnecessary to clean up after each study session, and to go through the process of "setting things up for study" at the beginning of each session.

Do not attempt to study in the same room you use for recreation.

If you have come to associate a room with relaxation, leisure conversation, or other forms of recreation, you will find that it will be difficult to develop the concentration you will need for serious study.

Don't compete with distractors.

Don't attempt to do serious study while the television or radio is on, while engaged in leisure conversation, or while other distractions are in the room. *Let the assignment be the only demand on your attention during a study session.* If you have seen other persons who seem to be able to attend to more than one thing at a time, it is likely that they have learned to shift rapidly their attention from one thing to another rather than to attend to many things at the same time. It is highly possible that even these persons lose something in shifting from one thing to another. Be on the safe side. Avoid competing with distractions or dividing your attention. Don't believe that soft music will help you to concentrate. It is more likely that it helps you to relax. If you need to relax do so before you begin serious study. Effective learning requires some tension—some concern.

Study for a particular course or lesson the same time each day if possible.

The habit of thinking about one subject at the same time each day fosters a mind set which is conducive to concentration. If, for example, you study your mathematics each day just before the mathematics class you will find that it will be easier for you to concentrate on mathematics during this period. Less effort will be required for you to keep your mind on mathematics.

Do not attempt to study while in a too relaxed position.

Do not attempt to do serious study while settled in a lounge chair or while lounging in an armchair. Be comfortable while studying, but avoid being too comfortable. Some physical tension is necessary for serious study and learning.

Avoid serious study immediately after a heavy meal.

The body tends to be in a relaxed state during this period and learning efficiency is not at its highest level. It has also been said that eating heavily just before study interferes with the proper use of one's mental efficiency. The explanation given is that over-eating causes a rush of blood to the stomach, and a recession of blood from the brain.

Do something while studying.

The most common, and, perhaps, the most useful activity is to write—make notes, underline important ideas in your book, check references to be consulted later, etc. The important thing is to *do something while you study*. The act of writing, for example, implies a reaction to something you have read or heard. If you write, you must have something to write. This requires that you do some thinking about the materials you have read or heard discussed. The act of thinking is the first step in actual study.

Spend enough time at study.

A general rule, as stated above, is to spend two hours in study for each hour spent in class each week. If a course requires that you attend class three hours per week, then spend *at least* six hours of study per week for this class. The "bright" student (one who has already developed a high degree of scholastic ability) may be able to get by with less, and the average or below-average student may need to spend much more time in study. Discover your own needs and act accordingly. Until you are sure of the amount of time you will need for study, devote at least two hours of study per week for each hour spent in class.

Begin studying immediately after you sit down at your study desk.

Don't permit yourself to "fool around." Begin immediately to do those things connected with your assignment. Open your books, read the assignment, get out your notes, begin to read. Concentration will soon come if you go through the act of studying. Hesitation or "fooling around" only invites mind wandering or daydreaming.

Set aside at least one hour per week for a review in each of your school subjects.

If you are taking four subjects, then set aside four hours (on your study schedule) for a review in these subjects each week. The purpose of these reviews is to re-learn and to over-learn the materials which have been studied during the week. During these reviews, consult your class notes, notes made in your books, and any other materials which have been a part of the class work during the week. Spend more time on those things which seem to be less clear to you or on those materials

DON'T ATTEMPT TOO MUCH

you may have completely forgotten. The review periods help you to better understand the materials covered in class, and to remember the things you learn for a longer period of time. Review periods also help you to keep alert for quizzes and examinations which may be given without warning.

Don't attempt to participate in too many out-of-class activities.
Do not attempt to carry too many activities outside of your class work regardless of how important you may consider these activities to be in terms of your over-all development. If you are playing on an intra-mural team, for example, don't tryout for a part in a dramatic presentation. Don't attempt to work on several committees during any one school year. This practice is especially important during your first year in school. Attempt only a few activities until you have found out how difficult school work is for you. School activities are a vital part of your education, but don't attempt to get this part of your education at the expense of your classwork.

Also, if you have to work at an outside job, carry fewer school subjects than you would otherwise. Make up your mind to spend a longer period of time in obtaining your education if work will interfere with your taking a normal class load. The most common cause of failure or poor work among college students is the attempt to carry a full load of class work while earning a living. The following table will give you some idea of how much you should attempt in the way of classes if you are working while going to school. However, the number of classes one can carry successfully while working depends upon a number of individual factors, including the aptitude of the student. The more scholastic aptitude one has, all else being education, but don't attempt to get this part of your education at the expense of your classwork. Maintain a sensible balance between class activities and out-of-class activities.

Number of hours you work per day	Number of credits you should carry
1 or 2	not over 15 semester hours
3 or 4	not over 12 semester hours
4 or more (or at night)	not over 10 semester hours

When in class pay attention to what is going on.

Make your time as profitable as possible. *Not only stay awake, but alert.* Keep thinking about what is being said. If there is a discussion, get into it. If there is a lecture, follow it closely to see how it "hangs together." Try to relate the present class work to that which has gone on previously. Also try to anticipate what is coming next. Don't assume that because the teacher does much of the talking, all that you have to do is to sit on a chair in front of him. Get all of the ideas you can while in class. Take every opportunity to express your own ideas. This is the best way to find out if your ideas are correct. Also, the act of expressing your ideas implies some thinking, and thinking is the basis of study and learning. Above all, *attend* class regularly, regardless of whether you are required to or not.

Recite often in class, and to yourself while studying.

Test your knowledge by taking every opportunity to recite in class. Also test your memory and understanding of what you read by closing the book and reciting to yourself. If there are gaps in your knowledge, or if your understanding of a topic is faulty, your teachers will discover it during your recitation and will help you to correct this misunderstanding. Likewise, by reciting to yourself and then checking your recitation against the materials you have just read in your book, you are testing your knowledge.

Make up illustrations.

Check on your understanding of a topic by thinking up your *own* illustrations. If you thoroughly understand a topic or an idea, you are able to illustrate it. If you can't think of illustrations other than those given by the book or by your teacher, it is a sign that you need to spend more time in relearning the topic.

Find some practical use for your newly acquired knowledge.

When you find some practical application for your new learning, you are increasing your chances for remembering the materials over a longer period of time. If, for example, you have just learned how to extract square root by using the slide

To which group do you belong?

rule, use this method in solving all problems involving square root, especially during the period immediately following this learning. This practical application makes it less likely that you will forget this use of the slide rule. Also, in the section of this book dealing with reading skills you will be given suggestions for increasing your reading speed. Begin to use these suggestions immediately in all of your reading assignments.

Early in each course you are pursuing, get an overall view of its content.

At the very beginning of each course get a bird's eye view of what will be in the course. You can get such a view by examining the table of contents of the text, browsing through the text, reading the introductions to parts of the text, and by reading the chapter summaries whenever they are provided. When you have some idea of what the whole course is about, then each part will be more meaningful to you. You will be better able to see how the entire course "hangs together."

Write down and prepare all assignments.

Write down each assignment immediately after the teacher gives it. Don't trust your memory. One section of your notebook should be reserved for assignments. Also make it a practice always to prepare the assignment before attending the next class. When you have done this, what goes on in class will have more meaning for you. You will have prepared a framework into which the class discussion will fit. In a sense, you have acquired "hooks" on which to hang what the instructor says in his lectures or discussions. You will have a better understanding of what he is attempting to put across to the class.

Get the habit of intending to learn.

Little learning takes place unless there is some *intent* on your part. When in class, pay close attention to what is going on. To give yourself some assurance that you will attend to what goes on in class, set up some definite purpose—something that you intend to gain from a class discussion. You may ask yourself such questions as these: what is the chief point of this discussion? What is the teacher "driving at"? In an attempt to get an answer to such questions, you will find yourself attending to what is being said. When one's attention is not sharply focused, what he hears, reads, or sees will make little impression, and the results will be hazy learning, or no learning at all.

Relate new learning to past experiences.

As far as possible, tie in your new knowledge with your past experiences. You are doing this when you attempt to illustrate your newly acquired knowledge. It is for this reason that illustrations are helpful in making new knowledge meaningful. Any experience to be meaningful must be linked with some past experience. Many times a new experience is not meaningful to students because the new experience assumes some past experience which the student may not have had. In this case, the only answer is to go back and learn the material that is pre-requisite for the new knowledge.

Distribute your learning efforts.

Don't attempt to learn a thing all at once, especially complex skills. Arrange several study sessions instead of an *unduly long* one. Don't study for too long a period of time at one sitting without introducing a rest pause or at least a change in the type of activity. How long you will be able to study at a time without impairing your mental efficiency depends upon your own characteristics. Some students will do well to study for half an hour, and then take a few minutes away from study. Others may find that they can concentrate for one hour without a break of some kind. In any case, do not study without these rest pauses. As a study session continues, you will get diminishing returns from your efforts. A five minute break will be better than none. If your schedule will not permit you to rest during these study breaks, then change to an activity that is as different as possible from the activity just finished. If, for example, you have been studying some difficult subject for an hour and do not wish to use the break for just resting, then engage in some activity that will not require a great deal of mental work. Experience has shown that intensive study for relatively short periods (1½ to 2 hours) followed by liberal periods of rest are most conducive to learning efficiently. Another reason for distributing learning effort is that acquiring new skills often requires the "falling out" or forgetting of old habits. This forgetting requires time. It is for this reason that most motor or muscular skills are acquired only after many practice periods covering days and, perhaps, months.

Do not study similar materials in succession.

Follow the study of one subject with a subject as much unlike the first subject as possible. If, for example, you will need to study mathematics, physics, literature, and English in one evening, don't study mathematics and physics in succession or English and literature together. It is better to study these subjects in this order: mathematics, literature, physics, and English. When you study materials involving similar content or similar skills one right after the other, forgetting is greater than it would be if you followed the study of one subject with an entirely different subject. The technical term used for this factor in forgetting is retroactive inhibition.

Whenever feasible, do important study just before sleep or recreation.

The rate of forgetting has been found to be reduced by sleeping or engaging in recreation immediately following serious or important study. The recreation should be of a type that involves little mental activity.

Practice the habit of overlearning.

When you have learned material to the point at which you can repeat or reproduce it without error, then go over these materials several times more. This additional time spent in going over the materials is overlearning. Overlearning is important in that it helps you retain what you learn for a longer period of time. This is the reason for frequent review of materials learned.

Engage in purposeful activity while working in the laboratory.

When working in the science laboratory, know what you are doing and what you are looking for. If you are to perform an experiment, read all about it even before you come to the laboratory. Read the instructions carefully. Know beforehand what outcome is expected from the experiment.

Pay close attention to graphs, drawings or tables.

Do not skip graphical materials in your reading. Learn to read diagrams of all kinds. These materials have a special purpose in the text. They are important because they summarize in a small amount of space certain facts and relationships that otherwise would require hundreds of words to express, and even then might not be clear.

Watch carefully for technical or new words when listening or reading.

Be sure that you learn the meaning of each new word you come across. You cannot afford to neglect the technical vocabulary of any subject as each word of this type stands for an idea which is important to know if you are to master the subject. Every course has such a fundamental vocabulary. When you come across such words in your reading, mark them in someway (circle or underline) to remind yourself that you are to consult the dictionary to obtain the meaning of the word. In this connection, when you come across a word for the first time don't stop at that point to look it up. The practice of stopping for each new word interferes with concentration and will result in your getting little from what you read. Try to guess the meaning of the word by the way it is used. Then when you have read the complete passage, stop to look up the new words in the passage. It is best to consult a technical dictionary when looking up words peculiar to a specific subject. Many subject matter fields have such a dictionary. If, for example, you come across the word "stimulus" while reading your psychology assignment, and you are not familiar with this word, it is better to look for its meaning in a psychological dictionary.

Use group study techniques.

Learning and reviewing in a give-and-take situation with others studying the same materials can be very helpful. Proceed as follows:

(1) Find three or four students (not too many) interested in group study.

(2) Reserve a library room (or other room—perhaps one at home) for several hours on certain dates.

(3) Assign each student a part of the material (chapter, section, etc.) for *intensive* study. Each student presents his materials orally (or orally and written) to the group.

(4) Each student prepares quiz questions for the other members. Exchange questions and practice taking tests. A question-and-answer session follows.

(5) Offer tutoring services to those having difficulty.

EXERCISE V

A. Make a list of all your good study habits.
B. Make a list of all your poor study habits.
C. For each poor study habit listed, indicate what *specific* plan you have to replace this poor habit with a good one.

SECTION V

Taking Notes

The notes you take on your lecture or reading assignments are basic guides in your study and learning. Your knowledge of the subjects you are studying is not likely to be any better than the notes you construct during the course of your study. Good notes have several specific functions.

They help you understand the teacher's or author's plan of presenting his materials.

They help you retain what you learn, with greater accuracy and for a longer period of time.

They provide you with concise and complete outlines for review, especially in preparing for examinations. Notes are also useful in the writing of a term paper or research report.

They help you in the preparation of your daily assignments.

They help you to concentrate on the materials the writer or speaker is presenting. Notetaking is a form of self recitation which promotes both concentration and retention. Good notetaking is an active process which requires thinking. Thinking is the basis of learning.

They help you identify the basic or essential materials in a course.

The following suggestions will help you take the kind of notes that will be of greatest use to you in all of your learning situations. Read these suggestions carefully, and incorporate them in your notetaking habits.

Take notes in all learning situations.

Your notes should include the essential materials or ideas gotten from your textbook, outside reading assignments, lectures, classroom discussions, field trips, film viewing, etc. All of these different kinds of experiences are provided as a means of promoting learning. Consider all of them as being important. Record the basic ideas secured from all learning situations.

Develop some simple, but usable system of "shorthand."

If you have already developed some skill in one of the standard systems of shorthand, then use it in your note-taking wherever feasible. If you are not so fortunate, work out some simple shorthand system of your own. Invent shortcuts. Use abbreviations, initials, short phrases, or other symbols to represent the ideas you wish to record in your notes. These ideas will come from your readings, lectures, class discussions, and other learning experiences. For example, use numerals instead of writing out numbers, use initials when referring to the names of important persons. Make use of such abbreviations as *re* for concerning, *e.g.* for example, *i.e.* for that is, etc. Also, make use of mathematical symbols such as the *plus* $(+)$ sign for *and,* the *equal* $(=)$ sign to indicate a relationship between certain ideas or propositions, and the *therefore* $(\therefore)$ symbol whenever indicating deduction or inference. A shorthand system reduces the time involved in writing complete sentences. In learning situations, you should spend most of your time in getting the *meaning* of the experience, and not in writing notes. One exception to the use of abbreviations is in the case of taking notes on materials which are highly technical. In technical materials, almost every word is "loaded" with meaning which is vital to an understanding of the sentences which follow. With such materials, it might be better to use phrases or complete sentences in your notes, especially if it is your first experience with the topic. This practice results in notes which will have greater meaning to you when you study your notes on technical materials. It is usually more difficult to "read between the lines" in technical materials than with materials of a more general nature.

Do not take notes which are too detailed.

Even with some system of shorthand, don't take notes in too much detail. The important thing to remember in note-taking is to record the *essential* facts or ideas, and *not all* the facts or ideas presented by the writer or speaker. The purpose of notes is to furnish you with clues which will help you recall relevant ideas when you review or study your notes. The effort required in taking notes which are too detailed will prevent you from concentrating on the *meaning* of the material the speaker or writer is presenting.

Assume an active meaning-seeking attitude when reading or listening.

Concentrate on getting the *meaning* out of your learning experiences. In reading, this practice will require that you get an overview of the purpose of the materials you will read before making any notes on them. This can be gained by scanning the materials, looking at section or topical headings, or by reading the summaries whenever they are provided.

Then in the more serious reading of the materials, set out to find answers to questions suggested by this initial scanning or summarizing. For example, the chapter heading in a book might be—"Basic Skills in Notetaking." Thumb through the chapter to see what topics or skills are discussed. Then on the serious reading of this chapter, your notes should list each of the skills discussed, and each skill listed should be followed with a condensed explanation of the skill or answers to such questions as: What is the meaning of this skill? How can it be acquired? Your notes on reading such a chapter might look something like this:

(1) Shorthand skills
   Shorthand—using initials, abbreviations, symbols.
   . . .
   Acquired—learn common abbreviations, meaning of symbols, etc.

(2) Condensing skills
   Condensing—rephrasing in own words . . .
   . acquired—to get *meaning* prior to notetaking . . .

Likewise if listening to a lecture on "Basic Skills in Note-taking," and the lecturer makes the statement "The skills important to notetaking are —," wait until he has given the skills before you start to take notes. If he states the skills before giving any explanations, then list the skills in the same order he gave them, and leave a space for writing a condensation of the explanations that he will give later. The lecturer might explain each skill mentioned before proceeding to name and discuss another skill. If this is the case, then your notes will follow the same order. That is, you will list a skill, follow it with a brief explanation of its meanings, before listing another skill. After class, you might want to revise these notes by writing down all these skills together so that you will be able to see them at a glance.

In assuming an active meaning-getting attitude, ask yourself such questions as Do I understand what I am reading or what is being said? What is this all about? Do I agree with it? Then proceed to condense the reading, lecture, or discussion by recording the "meat" of it in your notes.

Use your own words in notetaking.

After getting the meaning of what the speaker or writer has presented, then proceed to condense and rephrase it in your own words. During your review of these notes, your own words will have more meaning to you than will those of the speaker or writer. Then too, this practice is a test of whether you understand what the speaker or writer has presented. To rephrase something in your own words demands some understanding of the materials. The practice of rephrasing materials in your own words is a kind of self recitation which forces you to do some thinking about the materials. Thinking increases understanding. The net result will be that your learning will be more useful, and will be retained for a longer period of time.

Prepare for notetaking before going to class.

This not only means having necessary equipment such as pencils, a pen, and notebook, but it also involves reading or studying the assignment before class. This prior study helps you to anticipate what is coming and gives you a "framework" through which you will be able to get more meaning from the class lecture or discussion. This increased meaning secured from materials will result in more meaningful notes being taken.

Don't hurry your notes.

Good notes are both *readable* and *accurate*. Don't hurry your writing so that you will not be able to read it once it is "cold." The primary cause of hurried notes is an attempt to take notes which are too much in detail. Some persons write so frantically during class that not only will the writing be illegible, but there will have been so much concentration on writing that no meaning will have been obtained from the lecture or discussion. Check the accuracy of your lecture notes by comparing them with those of your classmates, or by consulting the teacher on points at which you have some doubt. If you miss a point while listening to a lecture, don't try to recover it at that moment. This may cause you to miss the next point being made by the speaker. Leave a blank space on the page and get the point from a classmate or from the speaker immediately after the lecture.

Notes should be neat and in good form.

Give each page of your notes a clear and accurate title. Also number each page of notes taken on a topic. This practice not only facilitates review by enabling you to quickly find wanted materials, but in case your notes get mixed up accidentally, you will know "what goes with what."

Leave a margin of about two inches on each page of notes. This will provide space for additions or corrections. When reviewing, you may also wish to indicate your reaction to the materials by writing brief notes at the appropriate place in the margin. For the same reason, it is also a good practice to take notes only on one side of the page. The reverse side can be reserved for additions, observations, or reactions.

It is usually a good practice to write notes in ink. Ink is more durable and is usually more easily read. If you are in the beginning stages of acquiring skill in notetaking, pencil notes might be better since these notes will have to be corrected or revised before being recorded in final form with ink. Don't impair the effectiveness of your notes by decorating the page with doodling. Idle drawings or figures imply that your attention was divided. For this reason, you may doubt the accuracy or completeness of your notes. Notes taken under such conditions are usually not very useful in reviewing. In addition, the drawings or figures on the page serve to distract you when attempting to review them. Concentrate on the learning experience at hand, and practice your art work at some other time.

Re-write or revise your notes as needed.

The ultimate goal in notetaking is to be able to take notes which do not need revising. However, until you have acquired such an ability, you may find the need to revise your notes daily. You may need to do further condensing of the notes you take in class, delete irrelevant materials, or add important points missed in the initial notetaking. Strive to improve your notetaking skill to the point where revisions will be unnecessary or where there will be a minimum of such revisions.

Organize and combine your notes.

All notes should be organized in a logical manner so as to show the proper relationship of facts recorded. For example, if notes concern steps or procedure in a process, then the steps should be listed in the same manner as they would naturally occur. Definitions should be placed in proximity to the word being defined. Likewise, notes from various sources, but on the same topic, should be combined. That is, combine notes on a topic that might have come from listening to a lecture, a class discussion, textbook or other reading, viewing a film, etc. These notes from various sources give fuller meaning to the topic, and should be placed together where they will not be overlooked when reviewing the topic. Some students make the mistake of having reading notes appear in one place in the notebook, lecture notes in another, chemistry notes on the same page with English notes, etc. Such practice not only leads to confusion, but renders your notes practically useless.

Use one notebook cover for all of your notes.

Keep notes on all of your subjects in *one loose-leaf* notebook. When you get the habit of carrying one notebook, you will be assured of always having notes you might need at a particular time. In attempting to keep up with many notebooks, you will often find that the notes you need might have been left at home through mistake. While you will keep notes on all subjects in one notebook, reserve a section in the notebook for each subject. Cardboard dividers will be needed to make the separations. Also reserve a section in this notebook for recording all assignments immediately when given. This is another reason for having the notebook with you at all times.

Keep special research or theme notes in a usable form.

In taking notes on your reading in preparation for writing a special research report or term paper, it is a good policy to place such notes on index cards. (Fig. 2) The size of the cards used will depend upon many factors such as the form of the notes—whether in outline or summary form, the number of cards needed, etc. However a 3 x 5 or 4 x 6 card is usually satisfactory, and makes for easy handling. Have one card for each reference source used. The card should contain the correct identification of the reference and the source from which it came. This will include the name of the author (s) , including the initials; the title of the book or article; the name of the publisher if a book; or if an article is cited, the name of the periodical in which it is found, including the volume and page number. The important part of the card, however, will contain your notes on your reading of the book or article. As in the case of all notetaking, the purpose is to record the *basic* or *essential* ideas presented.

Review your notes daily.

Review daily the notes from each class. Do this as soon after class as possible. This daily review of notes is in addition to the one hour that you will set aside for reviewing each subject each week.

SOME SUGGESTIONS FOR MAKING NOTES IN YOUR BOOK

The usefulness of your textbooks, and other *personal* books can be increased manyfold by making notes on materials as you read them. Such notes enable you to quickly find what you want when reviewing, and also serve to make important ideas stand out. This is important when reviewing for examinations, in preparation for writing themes or research reports, or in studying for daily assignments. There are no standard rules for making notes in your book. The important thing is to work out some system of notations that will be *meaningful* to you. One system of notations is given on page 57, and is illustrated in figure 3. However, you may want to modify these to fit your own needs. They are only suggestive.

In making notes in your books, observe the following basic principles:

Adopt a system of notations and stick to it.

Attempt to use a uniform system of notations. The symbols you choose to use must mean the same thing in all of your books. For example, if you choose to use the question mark "?" to indicate that you do not fully understand the passage where this symbol appears, then use this symbol to mean the same thing in all of your books. That is, it indicates that the materials are not clear to you. Don't use this same symbol "?" in another book to indicate disagreement with a passage.

Use a simple and practical system of notations.

As far as possible use symbols or abbreviations which are in common use. (Fig. 3) Also keep the number of symbols used at a minimum. If you make use of too many different symbols, you are likely to forget the intended meaning of some of them.

Get the overall meaning of a passage before taking any notes on it.

Don't begin to mark your book or chapter in a book until you have first read the materials to get the overall purpose or meaning. This is done on the first reading in which you are largely skimming. Begin your note making on the second reading. Your notes are to indicate the important ideas or materials. You won't know what these are until you have some idea of what the whole thing is about.

Use discrimination in the use of notetaking symbols.

Too much underlining defeats its purpose. The purpose of underlining is to mark important materials. It is not likely that all of the materials or even a greater portion of them will deserve underlining. Underline only the essential or key words. Refrain from underlining complete sentences. In the following sentences, for example, only the key words have been underlined:

"*Concentration* is not a power with which some are born and which others never gain. It is a *way of behaving* which *increases clearness* of the situation toward which we are reacting, and enables us to *respond in a dynamic fashion.*"

The "meat" of the above statement is that concentration is a way of behaving which enables us to respond in a dynamic fashion as a result of increased clearness of situations. Underlining in this case should be limited to the words which help make this idea stand out.

One method to use in deciding on what is important in a passage is to set up for yourself certain questions to be answered through reading the passage. These questions result from examining topical or paragraph headings, and then turning them into questions. For example, in the chapter heading— "Preparation for Examinations," several questions seem to be implied, such as, "What are the steps in preparing for an examination?", etc. After setting up such questions, read to find the answers. Then, the materials that provide the answers are the essential materials. They should be marked by under lining or by the use of some other notations. If, for example, the chapter discusses several steps in the preparation for examinations, you might underline each step or use numerals (1), (2), (3), etc. to identify these steps. In many cases, the author will have already indicated the importance of materials by the use of italics or numerals.

Also keep on lookout for what the author considers important. Usually clues are found in topical headings and introductory statements. If an introductory statement begins "The basic principles involved are . . . ," then read to discover these basic principles. When you find them, and if they have not already been marked by the use of italics, numerals, or in some other manner, then proceed to underline them, identify each with a numeral, or both. Also look for statements which seem to evaluate or define something. They usually begin—"This is important because . . .", "A basic principle is . . .", "Learning is a process in which . . .", etc. Mark such materials so that they will stand out when you review them.

Use pencil instead of ink when making notes in your book.

Less damage is likely to be done to your books when pencil is used. Also, you might wish to make changes in some of these notes after you have gained a fuller understanding of the materials.

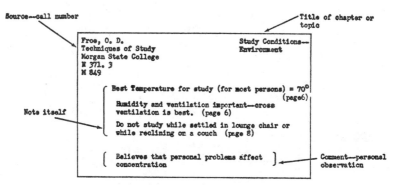

Fig. 2. Research Notes on an Index Card

SOME SUGGESTED SYMBOLS TO BE USED IN MAKING BOOK NOTES

|, ( ), [ ]   A vertical line in the margin, or a bracket, or parenthesis around a sentence or group of sentences is used to indicate an important idea or ideas.

___   Underlining is used to indicate especially important materials, specific points to be consulted during reviews, etc.

?   A question mark in the margin may be used to indicate that you do not understand the materials, or that the meaning is not fully clear to you.

O   A circle around a word may be used to indicate that you are not familiar with the word, and that you will come back later to look it up in the dictionary.

E   The letter "E" or a check mark (√) in the margin may be used to mark materials that are important and likely to be used as a part of the course examination.

1 , 2 , 3 , 4   Arabic numerals, circled or uncircled may be placed before a word or at the beginning of a sentence to indicate a series of facts, ideas, important dates, etc.

D   The letter "D" may be used to indicate your disagreement with a passage or a statement.

Keep in mind that effective notetaking is vital to learning. If your notes are effective, your learning is likely to be effective. Follow the suggestions given in this section, and strive to acquire the kinds of notetaking skills that will result in increased learning from your study efforts.

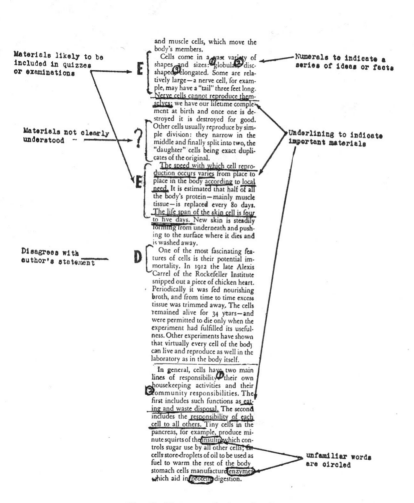

and muscle cells, which move the body's members.

Cells come in a vast variety of shapes and sizes: globular, disc-shaped, elongated. Some are relatively large—a nerve cell, for example, may have a "tail" three feet long. Nerve cells cannot reproduce themselves; we have our lifetime complement at birth and once one is destroyed it is destroyed for good. Other cells usually reproduce by simple division: they narrow in the middle and finally split into two, the "daughter" cells being exact duplicates of the original.

The speed with which cell reproduction occurs varies from place to place in the body according to local need. It is estimated that half of all the body's protein—mainly muscle tissue—is replaced every 80 days. The life span of the skin cell is four to five days. New skin is steadily forming from underneath and pushing to the surface where it dies and is washed away.

One of the most fascinating features of cells is their potential immortality. In 1912 the late Alexis Carrel of the Rockefeller Institute snipped out a piece of chicken heart. Periodically it was fed nourishing broth, and from time to time excess tissue was trimmed away. The cells remained alive for 34 years—and were permitted to die only when the experiment had fulfilled its usefulness. Other experiments have shown that virtually every cell of the body can live and reproduce as well in the laboratory as in the body itself.

In general, cells have two main lines of responsibility: their own housekeeping activities and their community responsibilities. The first includes such functions as eating and waste disposal. The second includes the responsibility of each cell to all others. Tiny cells in the pancreas, for example, produce minute squirts of the insulin which controls sugar use by all other cells; fat cells store droplets of oil to be used as fuel to warm the rest of the body; stomach cells manufacture enzymes which aid in process digestion.

Materials likely to be included in quizzes or examinations

Materials not clearly understood

Disagrees with author's statement

Numerals to indicate a series of ideas or facts

Underlining to indicate important materials

unfamiliar words are circled

Fig. 3. Notes made in a book

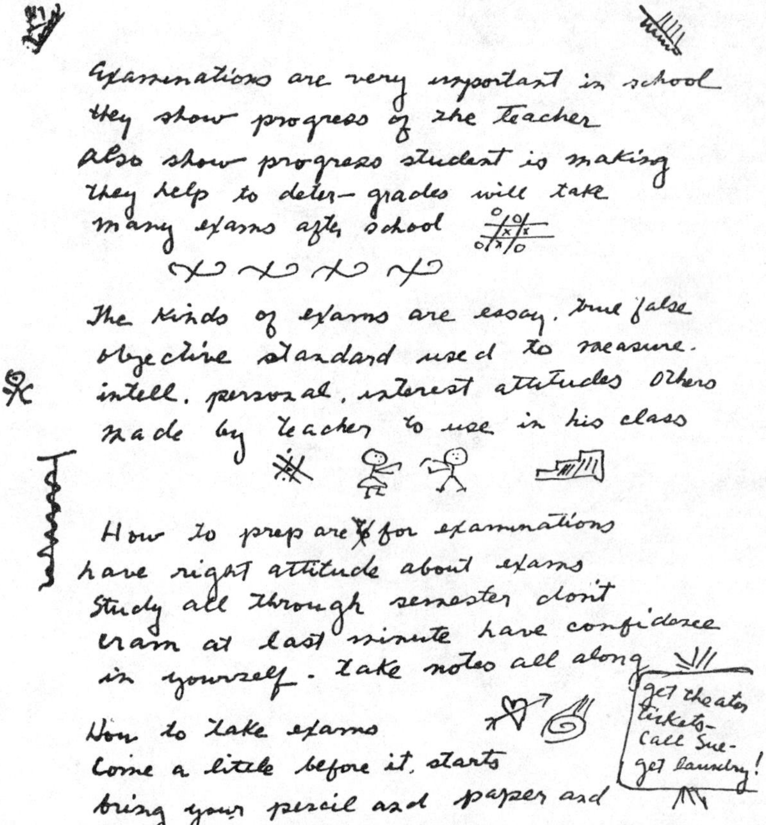

Examinations are very important in school
they show progress of the teacher
also show progress student is making
they help to deter— grades will take
many exams after school

The kinds of exams are essay, true false
objective standard used to measure.
intell. personal, interest attitudes others
made by teacher to use in his class

How to prepare for examinations
have right attitude about exams
study all through semester don't
cram at last minute have confidence
in yourself. Take notes all along

How to take exams
come a little before it starts
bring your pencil and paper and
all that you need
read the directions two times before start
Think about what you are going to write
before you begin and organize your
read all the questions before you
answer the first one

get theater
tickets—
Call Sue—
get laundry!

Fig. 4 Typical Notes of the Poor Student

Examination Skills

I. *Importance*
   (a) progress - tchr. - stdnt.
   (b) motivation
   (c) grades
   (d) after school

II. *Kinds*
   (a) essay
   (b) objective - standardized - intelligence
       personality - attitudes - interests
     1. true - false
     2. completion
     3. mult. - choice
     4. matching

III. *Preparing*
   (a) attitudes
   (b) reg. study - no cram.
   (c) good notes - review notes - underline text
   (d) weekly reviews - daily reviews
   (e) study with others

IV. *Taking Exams.*
   (a) on time - materials needed - direct.
   (b) overview → organize → write → proof read

Fig. 5. Typical Notes of the Good Student

EXERCISE VI

A. Make a list of all the things you find wrong with the notes in figure 4.

B. In one of your text books, make notes on a chapter by using symbols such as those suggested in this section.

Using the Library

The library may be viewed sentimentally as a repository of the wisdom of the ages, if you feel that way about it. To a student, however, the library is a tool which he uses to do his school work. Every student has to use libraries to get facts and information to complete oral and written assignments. If you know how to locate information quickly and efficiently in your school library you can save valuable time and effort.

A Bird's Eye View

Make a point of going to your school library and giving it the once-over to see what it has to offer you. Of course, all libraries have a main collection of books and periodicals for student use. In addition some libraries have special collections such as rare books and author collections. Or there may be a collection of recordings or paintings; or a browsing room; or a projection room where movies and film strips are shown; or microfilms and a microfilm reader. Obtain from a librarian or make a floor plan of your library including appropriate labels, in order that you will know exactly what services the library provides you and where you may find these services. Make a point of knowing where you may find the reference books and periodicals; what are the duties of the librarians and how you can use their services; what are the rules for charging books; what books and periodicals circulate and which do not; where the offices of the librarians are located; what are hours during which certain things can be done (such as viewing films and charging out certain kinds of books) ; what lectures, if any, by scholars and prominent persons the library sponsors; what exhibits the library maintains; and what kinds of information you can expect to get from the bulletin boards.

Services of the library.

The activities that take place in the library are designed to meet the needs of its users. It is in the *circulation* and *reference* departments that the public is served directly. The activities of the *circulation* department include giving assistance to persons in using the catalog (see section below), issuing and receiving books and other needed materials, and maintaining records of materials borrowed by the users of the library. The *reference* service in the library emphasizes *facts, information, ideas, interpretation,* and *personal aid.* It provides in person (and by telephone) practical information to be used immediately, and it provides especially the *materials* and resources needed in study, along with aid in using these materials. In the school library, reference work is closely tied to the curriculum and students are encouraged and guided in learning to do the work themselves.

The following pages in this section are designed to help you understand the usefulness of materials found in libraries, to teach you how to locate these materials, and to help you develop a facility for using all library resources with a maximum degree of independence. Do not hesitate to seek the help of library staff members.

The Classification of Books

Libraries contain many thousands (and sometimes millions) of books. Obviously there has to be some way of keeping up with them and locating them quickly. Therefore libraries arrange their books according to a system. There are a number of systems, but the one most commonly used is the Dewey Decimal System, devised by Melvil Dewey in 1876. Under this system ten broad classes include all books. Each class is assigned numbers as follows:

CLASS OF BOOKS (Materials)	NUMBER ASSIGNED
General Works (Generalities)	000
Philosophy and Related Disciplines	100
Religion	200
The Social Sciences	300

subdivided as follows:

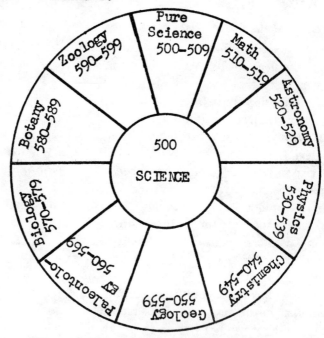

Fig. 6. Dewey Decimal System: Divisions in Science

Language	400
Pure Sciences	500
Technology (Applied Sciences)	600
The Arts	700
Literature and Rhetoric	800
General Geography, History, etc.	900

The system further divides each of the ten broad areas into ten subdivisions. For example, class 500 includes all works under science. (Fig. 6)
In turn, each of the subdivisions is divided into ten parts. For example, mathematics falls into the divisions indicated in figure 7.
Finally the system divides each "sub-subdivision" into ten classes and assigns each of them a decimal number. For example, arithmetic (511) is sub-divided 511.1, systems of

arithmetic; 511.2, fundamental rules of arithmetic; 511.3 prime numbers, and so on.

Another important classification system, used most often by very large libraries, is the *Library of Congress System*. This system combines the letters of the alphabet and Arabic numerals. An example of the letters assigned to broad classes of materials follows: *A*—General Works, *B*—Philosophy-Religion; *C*—History-Auxillary Sciences, etc. At present, all of the letters are not being used—*I, O, W, X,* and *Y* have been reserved for future expansion. Ask any librarian to explain this system to you in more detail, or obtain from a library a copy of the following: *Outline of the Library of Congress Classification.* This book can also be ordered from the U. S. Government Printing Office, Washington, D. C.

Using the card catalog.

Some libraries are changing to *book* catalogs, using *cards* only to *supplement* the book catalog—listing only the most recently published books on cards. Hereafter, when the term card catalog is mentioned in this book keep in mind this change, which you may find in some libraries.

The card catalog is the key to the use of the library. It allows you quickly and easily to locate all the books in the library. It contains on cards listed alphabetically the names of all authors of books the library possesses; the exact title of every book; the "call number" by which you or the librarian can locate the book; and subjects about which you can find information.

The card catalog consists of cabinets containing drawers in which you will find the cards. On the front of each drawer is an *outside label* to tell you at a glance the cards listed in it according to a strict alphabetical arrangement. In the drawing below, for example, the label on drawer 44 informs you that it contains cards falling from *u* to *z* after *st*. (Fig. 8)

Within the drawer there are *inside guides* to help you locate information in order that you will not have to thumb through a large number of cards to find one particular card. For

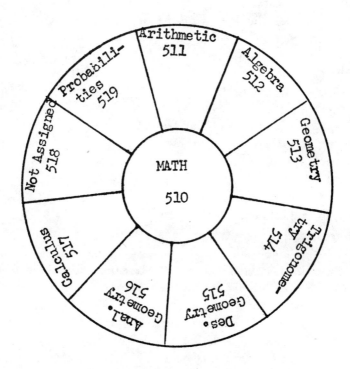

Fig. 7. Dewey Decimal System: Divisions in Mathematics

example, if you were looking up information about the American theater the inside label in the drawing below marked Theater will keep you from going through all the cards indicated by the outside label, TET-THEIQ. (Fig. 9)

You can locate books from three types of cards in the catalog. They are *author cards, title cards* and *subject cards*. See figures 10, 11, and 12.

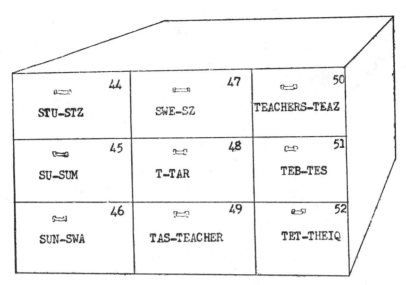

Fig. 8. A Card Catalog Cabinet

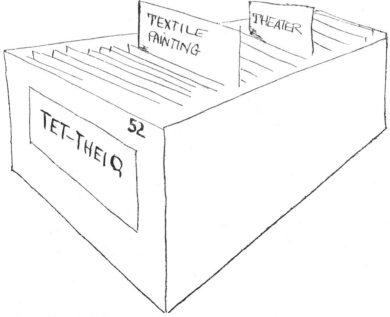

Fig. 9. A Card Catalog Cabinet Drawer with Inside Labels

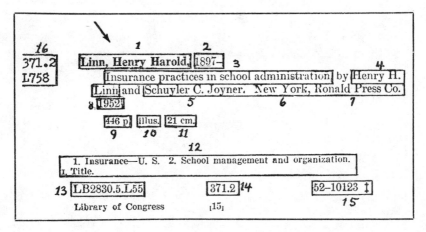

Fig. 10. Author Card

Key
1. Author's full name
2. Author's date of birth and indication by dash that he is still living
3. Title of the book
4. Author's name repeated to indicate he is co-author with
5. The second author
6. Place of publication
7. The publisher
8. Date of publication or copyright
9. Number of pages in book
10. Indicates the book is illustrated
11. Size of the book in centimeters
12. Contents of the book
13. Library of Congress classification
14. Dewey Decimal classification
15. Information for the librarian
16. Call number

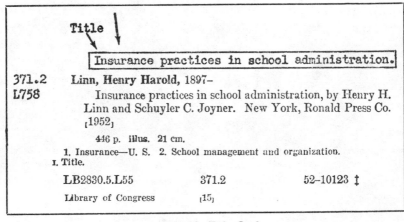

Fig. 11. Title Card

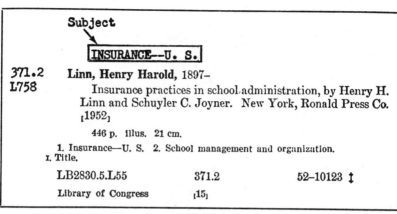

Fig. 12. Subject Card

You will see from the three cards that the information listed on each is exactly the same. The difference comes about in arrangement. The author's name comes first on the author's card; the title first on the title card; and the subject first on the subject card. By including the three types of cards the catalog makes it possible for you to locate a book if you know only the author, or the title, or the subject with which it is concerned.

Securing information from a card requires that you understand commonly used abbreviations. Some of the most frequently encountered are the following:

Abbreviation	Meaning
anon.	anonymous
bibl.	bibliography
cm.	centimeter
cf.	confer, compare
ch.	chapter
circ.	about, around (in time)
ff.	following
n.d.	no date
obs.	obsolete

Cross references

In addition to author, title and subject cards you will find cross reference cards. (Fig 13-a, b, c) The purpose of these cards is to direct you to additional sources from which you may get information.

ESKIMAU

See

ESKIMO

Fig. 13a. Cross Reference Card

A card as the one given above informs you that the information you seek is listed under two spellings. (Fig. 13a) In similar manner cross reference cards will direct you to two names an author might use: the type of card as indicated in figure 13b.

SAMUEL LANGHORNE CLEMENS

See also

MARK TWAIN

Fig. 13b. Cross Reference Card

Another type of cross reference card directs you to specific information under a general heading. See fig. 13c.

BOTANY

See Also

Flowers; flower culture; plants; plants cultivated

Fig. 13c. Cross Reference Card

Some Do's and Dont's for Using the Card Catalog

DON'T	DO
Look for titles that begin with articles: *a, an, the.* This applies to foreign titles as well as English	Look for a title by its first significant word: *Ventilation* for example, in the title, *The Ventilation of Small Homes*
Look for books written *by* an author to come last. Books written *about* the author come last; those he has written come first	Look up an author by his last name: Carver, William Harrison, for example
Look for titles that begin with numbers. Numbers are written out. Not *100 Days in Asia,* but *One Hundred Days in Asia*	Look for *Mac* instead of *Mc* in names beginning with one or the other. *Mc* is not used in the catalog.
Look for a professional or academic title as part of an author's name. Look, for example, for Einstein, Albert; not for Dr. Albert Einstein	Look for a professional title when it actually is the first word in the title of the book: *Father Sebastian—Worker of Miracles,* for example

USING REFERENCE BOOKS

The mainstay of successful study is the reference book. You are constantly on the search in school for biographical facts, data, quotations, information about countries, nations and races of people with which you prepare speeches, oral and written reports, classroom assignments, and get yourself in shape for examinations.

Encyclopedias.

An *encyclopedia* encompasses all phases of human knowledge. A *cyclopedia* is limited to a single branch of knowledge. However, the names are not absolute, as some cyclopedias bear the name of encyclopedias. If your task is to find general information of almost any kind, or facts about some one phase of human knowledge the encyclopedia is a good place to look.

Encyclopedias usually come in several volumes. Also they have indices, which are of great value to you. The importance of indices is due to the fact that they give you much more information than the alphabetical arrangement. You should always consult the index because only it gives you *all* the facts about locating information about a subject.

There are many encyclopedias at your disposal. Some recognized for their quality are the following:

Encyclopedia	Notes
Encyclopedia Americana	Has 30 volumes, and contains concisely written articles. A good source for general information. Volume 30 is the index.
Encyclopaedia Britannica	Has 24 volumes and tends to be more scholarly than the *Americana*. Indexed in Volume 24.
Compton's Pictured Encyclopedia	This familiar reference book has 15 volumes. In addition to articles it contains many pictures and illustrations, often beautifully done in color

If you want to find information in special fields of knowledge you should consult cyclopedias such as the following:

Special Field	Cyclopedias or Encyclopedias
Music	Pratt, W. S. *New Encyclopedia of Music and Musicians* Covers lives of musicians and facts about music
	Thompson, Oscar, *International Cyclopedia of Music and Musicians*
Applied Science	Hopkins, A. A. *Scientific American Cyclopedia of Formulas* Contains thousands of formulas and recipes
	Van Nostrand's Scientific Encyclopedia Includes astronomy, botany, chemistry, medicine, mathematics, and other branches of science.
Social Science	*Encyclopedia of the Social Sciences* Includes anthropology, education, law, politics and similar subjects
Allusions and Names	*Century Cyclopedia of Names* Names of persons, places, fictional characters, chronological tables of literature and history
Quotations	Hoyt, J. K. *New Cyclopedia of Practical Quotations* Contains quotations from ancient and modern writers

Atlases.

An atlas contains maps, information about countries, states, cities, and bodies of water. Also they indicate how names of places, rivers, mountains are pronounced, and give you directions for locating places on maps. Some good atlases are:

Goode, J. P. *School Atlas: Physical, Political and Economic*
Hammond, C. S. *Pictorial Atlas of the World*
Rand McNally World Atlas

Yearbooks.

Ever changing events demand that new information be constantly acquired. Yearbooks as the following keep you abreast of the times:

Yearbook	Notes
American Yearbook	Includes annual advances in art, business, education, and in practically all other important aspects of American life
Statistical Abstract of the United States	Includes data concerning numerous phases of American life: climate, manufacturing, finance, etc.
World Almanac and Book of Facts	Probably the most frequently consulted yearbook. Contains an enormous amount of data and other factual materials

Indices.

Indices permit you to find books published on some subject, or articles published in journals and magazines. Some indices list all published books or articles, others are confined to special fields.

Index	Notes
The United States Catalog	Lists books published in the United States by author, title and subject. Although this reference book is basically a librarian's book you will find it and its supplements useful in locating books not listed in your school library catalog

Reader's Guide to Periodical Literature	Indexes by author and subject articles which appear in approximately 100 magazines. Published every two weeks except during July and August, when it is published monthly. Through the *Guide* you can locate articles published as long ago as 1900
Education Index	Indexes articles and studies in the field of education
Agricultural Index	Helps you locate articles relating to agriculture and its branches
Art Index	Tells where you can find articles written about art

Biography.

Many reference works, including encyclopedias and dictionaries, give information about persons. However, you will find much more detailed information if you will consult a biographical dictionary.

Biographical Dictionary	Notes
Dictionary of American Biography	Contains information about important Americans who are dead. Has biographical sketches of artists, poets, soldiers, statesmen, inventors, from the time the country was founded
Dictionary of National Biography	Contains biographical sketches of Englishmen who are no longer living
Who's Who	Includes biographical sketches of important living Englishmen

Who's Who in America   Contains information about the birth, education and accomplishments of important living Americans

CHECK LIST

Check in Column 2 below whether your school library has the services listed in Column 1. In Column 3 write brief notes describing how you can make best use of the services provided:

1 Service	2 Yes or No	3 How the Service Can Help You
Browsing Room		
Special Author Collection (s)		
Movie or Film Strip Projection		
Microfilm Reader and Microfilms		
Collection of Recordings		
Historical or Art Collections		
Bulletin Board (s)		
Reference Librarian (s)		
Special Study Rooms or Carrels		
Loan Service with Other Libraries		
Lectures by Prominent Persons		
Reserved Books		
Other Kinds of Services (List them)		

EXERCISE VII

Use the information given you above in working out the following practice exercises.

A. The Card Catalog

1. Find the publisher and the date of copyright or publication of Thomas Hardy, *Return of the Native.*
2. What is the full name of the author of *Don Quixote?*
3. Find the author and title of a book under the general subject of semantics.
4. What, exactly, does the number 371.2 indicate on the author card given on page 66 above?
5. Find a book written about President John F. Kennedy.

B. Encyclopedias

6. Describe the interior of the Carlsbad Caverns.
7. Find a few facts about the Appian Way.
8. Name a few things characteristic of Stoicism.
9. Find a few facts about the Taj Mahal.
10. Find the title of one musical compositon by Paganini.
11. What symphony did Beethoven compose after he became deaf?
12. Find two common scientific formulas used in pharmacy.
13. Find the names of two constellations in the skies.
14. What was the name of the first Chief Justice of the United States Supreme Court?
15. What was the name of the second fictional country visited by Gulliver in Jonathan Swift's *Gulliver's Travels?*
16. What English poet wrote these words: "A little learning is a dangerous thing"?

C. Atlases

17. Find the name of one mountain range in or near Afghanistan.
18. Through what countries does the Amazon River flow?
19. What is the population of Calcutta?
20. What is the Great Divide, and where is it located?
21. Find a few facts about the Tigris River.

D. Yearbooks

22. Where is the National Statuary Hall located? In what year was it created?
23. How many American cities had populations of more than one million in 1970?
24. Locate a list of heads of states and prime ministers as of 1970.

25. In what year was penicillin discovered?
26. Find some information about the use of computers in America in 1970.

E. INDICES

27. Find the exact title and name of the author of an article about astronauts that appeared in *Esquire* Magazine, Volume 74, September 1970.
28. What is the title of an article by Clive Gammon that appeared in *Sports Illustrated* Magazine in October, 1970?
29. List the *title* and *author* of an article about *secondary education* published during 1971 and the *name of the periodical* in which it appeared.
30. Locate an article on Italian painting published during 1969.

F. BIOGRAPHY

31. What was the birthdate of the American poet, Edgar Allen Poe?
32. Find a few facts about the 19th century American painter, Benjamin West.
33. What was the 19th century Englishman, Benjamin Disraeli, noted for?
34. Name some of the achievements of the American scientist, Robert Oppenheimer.
35. What was the birthdate of Winston Churchill?

ARE YOU A
RAPID
READER ?

BOOKS FINISHED

BOOKS TO READ

OR
SLOW
READER ?

BOOKS FINISHED

BOOKS TO READ

JACK
WHITE

Building Reading Skills

Face this fact.

From 75 to 90 per cent of assigned school work requires you to read. This fact leads to one clear conclusion: the more efficiently you can read the better are your chances of becoming a successful student. Many students think that they can read better than they actually do. As a result they stumble along in their courses because they have limited vocabularies, or slow rates of reading, or difficulty in comprehending.

BUILD UP YOUR VOCABULARY

If your understanding of words is limited you will have great difficulty in grasping the author's "message." However, if you know what words mean you can read right along with ease and understanding.

Mastering the Dictionary.

The first step in building your vocabulary is to buy a good abridged dictionary, if you do not have one, and master its use. For practical purposes the abridged, or shortened, dictionary is best for study and reading since you can carry it around wherever you go. Choosing a dictionary is, similar to choosing a friend, a matter of individual preference. Certain questions will help you select a good one: is the dictionary of recent publication? Are the editors well-known persons in their fields? Are the entries clearly written? Are definitions easy to understand? Does the book have a thumb-index for finding words quickly? Does it list key words at the bottom of the page to speed up understanding pronunciations? Some of the better abridged dictionaries from which you can choose are *Webster's New Collegiate Dictionary; College Standard Dictionary;*

American College Dictionary; and *Webster's New World Dictionary.* Do not buy a little pocket dictionary as it is too limited to be of much use in serious reading and study.

The dictionary helps you 1) determine the meaning of a word; 2) learn how to pronounce it; 3) master its spelling; 4) become acquainted with its history; 5) become familiar with its part of speech; 6) secure facts concerning its usage among different regions and classes of people. In addition, in various other ways, dictionaries give you valuable general information and facts needed in reading and writing: the use of punctuation and mechanics; information concerning how to write a letter; facts relating to preparing a manuscript for publication: common non-verbal symbols used in mathematics, commerce, and other fields of knowledge, etc. Dictionaries differ in the kinds of general information they contain and kinds of symbols they use. This fact implies that you need to know thoroughly your own dictionary in order that you may make full use of its resources.

Your dictionary lists words alphabetically to help you find them easily. You should keep in mind that the listing is *strictly* alphabetical. Often words that are closely related in meaning do not follow one another in direct order. For example, *choke* and *choker* are closely related in meaning. However, one dictionary lists the following six words between them: chokeberry, choke-bore, choke-cherry, choke-coil, choke-damp, and choke-full. Observe how each of these words falls into correct alphabetical order between the final *e* in *choke* and the final *r* in *choker.* Because the dictionary sticks to a strict alphabetical order you may find that words closely related in meaning might not follow each other in immediate succession.

When you look up a word you should look for the *base* word and not its grammatical derivative. (A grammatical derivative is a syllable or ending added to the *base* to indicate change in grammatical form, such as *ed* for the past tense, or *ing* for the participle.) For example, if you are looking up *costuming* or *costumed* you would go about finding *costume,* the base word, and following it you would find verb forms ending in *ed* and *ing.* However, in *costumer* the final *er* is not a grammatical ending such as *ed* or *ing*. It is a suffix which modifies the word to mean "one who costumes." Since the *er* does not have a grammatical function as *ed* or *ing,* the word *costumer* is listed separately.

Dictionaries contain a pronunciation key to show you how to pronounce words. Certain marks called diacritical marks indicate just how vowels and consonants should be sounded: ā (as in able), ă (as in at), ä (as in art), for example. These diacritical marks differ in various dictionaries. Also a symbol (′) is given to show you where to give stress to syllables that must be pronounced with greater prominence than others. Since you have not mastered a word until you know accurately how it is pronounced in addition to its history, meaning, and usage you should study the pronunciation key thoroughly and refer to it when looking up words whose pronunciation is not clear to you. Most dictionaries also include key words at the bottom of the page which enable you to glance down at them to determine what sound a particular diacritical mark represents.

Your dictionary uses a kind of shorthand which you must understand in order to make full sense of its entries. This shorthand varies from dictionary to dictionary. The following in the American College Dictionary is illustrative: *n* for noun; *v.t.* for transitive verb; *adj.* for adjective, to represent parts of ‑speech. *Obs.* for obsolete, *colloq.* for colloquial, to represent usages of words; G for Greek, L for Latin, M for Mexican, to represent from what languages words came into English. In addition, the dictionary uses certain symbols that you must become acquainted with: *g* meaning going back to; *t* meaning taken from; *b* meaning a blend of. Since symbols differ in various dictionaries, you need a full understanding of all symbols in the dictionary you select for your own use.

Exercises in Using the Dictionary

Find the following information in your dictionary:

1.

On the lines at the right re-write the following words to indicate where and how they should be syllabicated, accented, and pronounced:

emphasize (example)	ĕm'fa sīz'
inimitable	
gesticulate	
insomnia	
mathematics	
susceptible	
squeegee	
Paleolithic	

2.

Write a key word on the line at the right which contains the underlined vowel sounds in each of the following words:

arid	
abaca	
Basil	
economy	
edible	
finagle	
final	
osprey	
Osage	
orthodox	
Ursa	
usury	

3.

On the line write a key word which will tell how the *c* or *ch* in each of the following words should be pronounced.

cello	_____	chantry	_____
charitable	_____	chaos	_____
chrism	_____	chameleon	_____
Charon	_____	Cebu	_____

4.

Find answers from your dictionary for as many of the following questions as you can:
1. What do the symbols A.A. U.P. represent?
2. Why was the name Baltimore oriole selected for this bird?
3. What is the chemical name for banana oil?
4. Find a synonym for *adscititious* in the following sentence: He included *adscititious* data.
5. What does the prefix *pyo* indicate in such words as *pyogenic* and *pyoid?*
6. How should dates be written in formal invitations?
7. Is *parlance,* meaning a talk or parley, in current usage?
8. What symbol is used in biology to represent a specified trait?
9. What special meaning does *abandon* have in the field of law?
10. What is the origin of the word *tantalize?*
11. From what language did *cruller* originate?
12. What is the difference in meaning between *exodus* and *emigrate?*

Analyzing words.

A second step in building your vocabulary is to master common roots of English words that have been taken from Greek and Latin. You can often unlock the meaning of a word if you recognize the basic meaning given it by its Greek or Latin root. For example, one common Greek root is *phon* referring to sound. If you know this you will be put on the right track in grasping the meaning of *phoneme* (smallest class of sounds in a language), or *phonemics* (the science of sound systems in a language). If, also, you can recognize another common word element taken from Greek, *gram* (meaning something written or drawn) the compound word

phonogram (a written symbol standing for a speech sound) will reveal much of its own meaning.

Some common Greek and Latin roots which give English words their basic meanings are the following: (Look up the words whose meanings you do not know)

ROOT	MEANING	EXAMPLE IN ENGLISH WORDS
acer	sharp	acerbity, acrimonious
ambulare	walk	ambulatory, ambulate
aer	air	aerie, aeriferous
brevis	short	brevity
cantare	sing	cantata, canticle
dominus	master	dominate, dominium
dormire	sleep	dormitory, dormant
fortis	strong	fortify
frater	brother	fraternal, fraternize
geo	the earth	geography, geocentric
mitto, missere	send	remit, missile
potior	strong, to be able	potent, potential

Basic meanings of roots are modified by *prefixes* and *suffixes*. Prefixes *add to* or *qualify* meaning. Suffixes indicate *function* or *behavior*. Common prefixes that you should know are the following:

PREFIX	MEANING GIVEN TO ROOT	EXAMPLE
a or ab	away from or absent	abscond, avert
a or an	not, without	atypical, anesthetic
ante	before	antebellum, anteroom
anti	against	antibody, anti-social
circum	around	circumnavigate, circum-scribe
com, con	with	compare, confer
contra	against	contrary, contravene
de	downward	descend, degrade
di, dis	apart from	divide, disappear

e, ex	out, out of	emit, expectorate
hyper	above, excessive	hypertonic, hypersensitive
hypo	under, beneath	hypodermic
inter	between	interpose, intervene
intra	inside	intramural, intracranial
intro	place before	introduce
per	through	permeate, perceive
pre	before	prefix, pre-judge
sym, syn	together	sympathize, synchronize
super	above	supervise, super-ego
trans	across	transact, trans-continental

Functions expressed by suffixes are classified below. Some may express more than one kind of meaning, and are placed in more than one classification.

Suffixes indicating belonging to, adhering to, pertaining to.

ac: as in *maniac*
an: as in *Georgian*
al: as in *constitutional*
er: as in *Marylander*
ic: as in *patriotic*

Suffixes indicating an action, a state or quality, condition, the practice of.

ance, ence: as in *appearance, prominence*
cy: as in *democracy*
dom: as in *martyrdom*
hood: as in *brotherhood*
ion: as in *partition*
ism: as in *Communism*
ist: as in *atheist*
ness: as in *kindness*
ry: as in *dentistry*
ty: as in *fidelity*

Suffix indicating a collection of persons, rank.

dom: as in *officialdom*

Suffixes indicating one who does something, an agent.

ant: as in *servant*
ent: as in *dependent*
er: as in *miner*
or: as in *tailor*

Suffix indicating a person associated with.

ite: as in *laborite*

Suffix indicating to follow some course of action.

ize: as in *economize*

Suffix indicating a place.

ate: as in *consulate*
ium: as in *auditorium*

Suffixes indicating that someone causes something to happen.

ate: as in *decorate*
fy: as in *solidify*

Suffixes showing ability, tendency to, worthiness of.

able: as in *portable*
ible: as in *permissible*
ive: as in *active*

Suffix indicating persons charged with some duty or responsibility, of the product of some duty or action.

ate: as in *magistrate, mandate*

Suffix indicating an inflammation of.

itis: as in *appendicitis*

Suffix indicating full of, characterized by, having.

eous, ious, ous: as in *gorgeous, serious, mucous*

Exercises in Building Word Meanings
from Roots, Prefixes, and Suffixes

A list of common roots is given below. Attach prefixes and suffixes to them which will give the meanings indicated.

duce, duct, to lead

One who leads away
to lead downward
to lead or move by persuasion
capable of being led or bent
one who leads a band

vert, turn

turn apart from
turn inward
turn against
turn toward

credo, believe

capable of being believed
not capable of being believed

dermis, skin

instrument for going beneath the skin
the top layer of skin

scribe, write

write beneath
write into
one who writes the notes of a meeting
write before

theos, god

study of religion
one whose beliefs are away from God
one who believes in many gods
one who believes in one God

aqua, water

a place where water is kept for creatures of the sea
pertaining to water
containing water or watery

Build your vocabulary according to a system.

A strong, active vocabulary does not develop by and of itself. You need to devise some kind of systematic attack upon
the problem of making your word stock grow. Some students
develop a card system. When they come across a new word they
write it on a note card, together with its pronunciation, meanings, synonyms and antonyms. Also they write short sentences
in which the new word appears in order that they may fix it
in their minds. Then they file the word cards alphabetically,

and review them at intervals. In case the word has an interesting history such information is also recorded.

Other students keep a notebook in which they record new words, their definitions, and examples of their uses. They review the new words periodically, and when possible they make a point of using them in speaking or writing.

If the materials are yours that you read you may find it helpful to underline new words that you come across. Words that are especially difficult you should underline two or three times to help fix them in your mind. Such systematic habits as these are rewarded. In a surprisingly short time you may find that your power of recognizing words has increased so that you will experience little difficulty with unfamiliar words when reading.

DEVELOP YOUR RATE OF READING

If you are going to cover the large amount of materials you have to read in school you must step up your rate of reading unless you are a fairly fast reader to begin with. Some students have the idea that they have to poke slowly along the lines to comprehend what the author is saying. While this may be true in reading some kinds of materials such as mathematics, in general reading it is far from the truth. As a rule, persons who comprehend best are, at the same time, quite rapid readers. Rapid reading serves three very practical purposes: it is a great time saver; it is an aid to concentration, since when you speed up the process you challenge your mind to perform its tasks rapidly and well; it helps to increase interest in reading, since by having the ability to cover a large amount of materials in a comparatively short period of time you will find the whole reading act stimulating.

One reason for slow reading is habits of slow perception. When you read your eyes begin at the left of the line and go across it in a series of swift hops. Each time they pause your eyes recognize symbols, blend them, and transmit an image to the "language center" in your brain. The image stimulates your brain to associate things in your experience with the symbols and you acquire "meaning." The mature reader takes in a comparatively large number of symbols each time his eyes pause, while the immature reader blends and transmits a small number. Also the mature reader allows his eyes to pause only a brief fraction of a second to perceive and transmit symbols, and once he has started he does not often go back along the line to get something he has missed. The immature reader, on the other hand, lets his eyes linger longer, and he often regresses. The fact is evident that the reader who has a wide recognition span, who "fixates" very briefly, and who regresses seldom is capable of reading much faster than his opposite number. If you are a slow reader you can step up your rate by training yourself to secure efficient perceptual habits.

One way to do this is to determine, first of all, what your average rate of reading is now. Select two or three passages from some fairly simple materials such as you will find in the *Reader's Digest*. Have someone time you when you begin to read each passage and stop you at the end of one minute. Count the number of words you read in each passage during the minute, and make an average from the two or three exercises. This will give you some idea about your average rate in words read per minute. If your average is from 300 to 350 your rate is about what you can expect from the ordinary reader for fairly easy materials. If it is much less plainly you need to do something about it. Even if your rate is more than 300 or 350 you can still improve it. Some persons have trained themselves to read at 1000 or more words per minute. Think of the time saved when contrasted with a rate of 300 or less!

You can build up your rate by subjecting yourself to a self-analysis. Do you vocalize when reading silently? That is, do you tend to move your lips, or pronounce words to yourself? Do you point with your pencil or finger when reading? Such habits slow down the movement of your eyes across the lines. You can help yourself overcome habits of vocalizing by holding your tongue between your teeth when reading. This prevents to some extent your vocal apparatus from acting. If you have the habit of finger or pencil pointing, keep your hands off the page (maybe in your pocket) until you overcome the habit.

Can you see all right? Many students neglect having corrected common visual defects such as short-sightedness, far-sightedness, astigmatism, and muscular imbalance. Reading requires a large amount of work by your eyes. If you are easily fatigued when reading, or the letters seem to run together, or you have difficulty in focusing, see an eye specialist.

You can develop your rate of reading by systematic practice. Choose some fairly easy materials to begin with, such as a story or simple novel, and practice letting your eyes move across the lines taking in broad thought units. Let your eyes pause between the slanted lines in the sample below.

Not this way:

You/ can/ learn /to/ read /fas /ter/ if/you /al/ low/

your /eyes /to /take/ in/large/ thought/ units /

This way is better:

You can/ learn to/ read faster/ if you/ allow/

your eyes / to take in/ large thought/ units/

This is still better:

You can learn to / read faster/ if you allow/

your eyes to/ take in/ large thought units/

Do not worry too much about comprehension to start with, because you know you can understand the easy materials you have selected. You are trying to break down old habits of slow eye movement, and establish swift habits. Later, when you feel that you can move your eyes swiftly, select more difficult materials and try to keep your swift eye movements while centering your attention on comprehending well what you read. There are numerous books (and courses) aimed at helping you improve your reading rate and comprehension. Ask your English teacher, counselor, or some other reliable person with knowledge in this area to suggest one to you. There are many materials for sale which claim to improve reading skills, that really have little or no value at all. The important thing is to get professional help in diagnosing your reading difficulties. These professionals may involve an eye specialist (M.D.), a psychologist, a reading specialist, or some other qualified professional person.

Many school centers provide reading clinics. These clinic

and laboratories are equipped with mechanical devices and special reading films to help you develop your reading skills. If a reading clinic or laboratory is in your neighborhood it might be to your advantage to investigate it to find out if its services are available to you. Be sure that the clinic or laboratory has been certified (accredited) by some reputable agency, such as the state or city Department of Education.

DEVELOP YOUR ABILITIES TO COMPREHEND

Vocabulary improvement, rate of reading improvement are only tools to the ultimate purpose of the reading act: comprehending what the author has to say. When you *comprehend* what you read you have been successful in receiving and retaining the author's message.

Comprehension is a multiple activity. It involves

Comprehending the meanings of words.

Some words "say" exactly what they mean: sharp knife, for example. When words are this familiar you have little trouble in grasping them. However, in comprehending *eleemosynary institution* you will probably have to get from the dictionary a synonym for *eleemosynary*. Other words suggest meanings apart from what they actually "say."

For example, if a friend of yours was lucky in a bridge game you might say, "My friend is *hot* tonight." Obviously you would not mean by *hot* that your friend has a high temperature. Words get meanings from *contexts*. You often comprehend the meaning of a word from its relations to other words around it. For example, if I were to say, "My sister bought a pair of comfortable *mules* today," you would guess that *mules* refers to footwear and not animals because of clues you get from *bought* and *comfortable*. Because words get their meanings from context and contexts constantly change you have to be prepared to follow shifts in meanings. For example, observe how the meaning of *dip* shifts in the following sentences: The old lady *dips* snuff. The stock market took a sudden *dip*. We ran across a *dip* in the road.

Keep in mind that the literal (or exact, or strict) meaning is often not the important thing. Often words convey their meanings indirectly. That is, they "say" one thing, but their real message comes out in what they imply. In "The marksman has a dead eye," *dead eye,* in all likelihood, would not mean lifeless. (What does it mean?) Getting implied meanings is simple when things and acts referred to are within easy grasp. They become more difficult when things, acts, and qualities are not within your range of experience. For example, "Ours was a Pyrrhic victory" might send you to the dictionary to find out what *Pyrrhic* means in order to get the meaning of *victory* that is intended. (What does *victory* mean in the sentence?)

In the study of materials in the content subjects you constantly run across technical terms. In comprehending such terms you have to understand that they refer to precise operations, objects and phenomena in those fields. Put them in another field and they mean something quite different. For example, *root* in mathematics means a quality which, when multiplied by itself a certain number of times, produces a given quantity; in botany it means a body of a plant which grows downward into the soil; in physiology it means the embedded or basal portion of a hair, tooth, or nail; in grammar and language it means the element of a compound word, as we have seen above. In general speech *root* has no technical meaning at all: "Money is the *root* of all evil," for example.

One practical way to master technical terms in your reading is to go through the assignment in the text or other materials and underline all terms that you do not know. Then, before, you begin reading, look up these terms in the glossary that may be provided in the text, or in vocabularies that are specially written for some subject fields, such as science or mathematics. In case neither of these sources are at hand, your dictionary will help you, although it is better to depend upon more specialized sources. Concentrate, especially, upon the thing, or operation, or quality that the term refers to, and fix it clearly in your mind. It will also help to list these terms on cards or in a notebook, together with their meanings and notes on how they originated, and their pronunciations. Periodic reviews of your terms will help to fix them in your memory. A specimen card follows:

Term: *ptyalin*   Pronounced: tī'-à-lĭn
Subject field: Biochemistry from Greek *ptalyon,* meaning spittle; thing and operation: enzyme in saliva that changes starch into dextrin and maltose

A note card as the above pre-supposes, of course, that other terms included in it are already known to you: enzyme, dextrin, and maltose. If not, you should master them the same way you mastered *ptyalin.*

Comprehending sentences.

Words are the building blocks of the author's message. However, the actual unit through which he converses with you is the sentence. That is, the author so combines words into sentences that they produce *units* of information, thought, and idea. You comprehend sentences in two ways: one is through a grasp of what the author actually "says." You comprehend the meaning of individual words, relate them, and come out with the precise, strict bit of information or idea that the author wants you to come out with. When the words in the sentence are familiar comprehending is simple: "I see a cow," for example. If the same bit of information is expressed this way, "Within my purview is a ruminant of the genus *Bos,*" you probably will have to use the dictionary to find synonyms for the unfamiliar words. The second way by which you comprehend sentences is through inference. That is, the author suggests things that he does not actually "say." You have to understand him by "reading between the lines." For example, in a passage dealing with freshmen theme writing an author said the following: "To prove that people do think and have ideas there are the contributors to Dorothy Doe's column." In comprehending this sentence there are several things you have to "read between the lines" that are not actually said: people do express their ideas to Dorothy Doe; Dorothy Doe is Dorothy Dix, newspaper writer, or some other writer who deals with certain problems of people; that the things people write to Dorothy Doe about are love and marriage problems. You have to go to your *experience* to supply the missing links. Sometimes feeling reactions are involved in inference: "My roommate is a snake," for example. You can sense that whoever said these words probably had feelings of dislike, that the tone he uses is sarcastic, and that it is likely that he desires other people to feel toward his roommate as he does.

Comprehending paragraphs.

Authors put sentences together in paragraphs to form large units of an entire composition. You comprehend paragraphs principally through their structure. They present a central idea and details that support and bring out the central idea. Your task is to recognize the sentence that presents the main idea, usually the topic sentence. The topic sentence most often is found at the beginning of the paragraph (although not always) and signals to you that here is the main thought that is developed in this paragraph. Through processes of comparing and contrasting, defining, illustrating, giving details, etc. the author supports in other sentences the main idea expressed in the topic sentence. Your job as reader is to grasp the main idea, and relate the other sentences to it in such a way that you grasp the aspect of meaning presented by the paragraph as a whole.

Typical structure of a paragraph developed by details.

(1) Licorice is at once the most mysterious and the most familiar of plants. (2) The use and refinement of this sweet root have followed the march of civilization. (3) Licorice was treasured by ancient man. (4) In China the Buddhist priests used a liquid extracted from it in their ceremonies. (5) The Scythians discovered that licorice quenched thirst: legend had it that Scythian warriors could go for twelve days without drink when supplied with licorice and mare's milk cheese.[1]

Analysis: Sentence 1 is the topic sentence and states the main idea.

Sentences 2 and 3 give details showing the familiarity of licorice, as announced in sentence 1.

Sentences 4 and 5 give details showing that licorice is mysterious, as announced in sentence 1.

[1] William H. Walker, "Licorice: Dark Mystery of Industry," *The Atlantic Monthly* (November, 1952).

Comprehending the whole composition.

The ultimate job in comprehending words, sentences, and paragraphs is, of course, comprehending a whole composition, whether it be an article in a magazine or a chapter in a book. Comprehending the whole composition requires a grasp of its structure. Certain paragraphs do special jobs within the composition. The *introductory paragraph* either tells you in plain terms what the author is going to write about, or implies it, or sets up a mood that is developed in the remainder of the composition. *Transitional paragraphs*, most often very short, carry you over, so to speak, from one aspect of the author's thought to another. *Summarizing paragraphs* restate in some way or another what the composition as a whole has developed.

The author has some kind of purpose in mind when he writes a composition. It is up to you to grasp his purpose. It may be that he writes to give you facts and information; or to criticize manners and morals; or to argue the correctness or incorrectness of a point of view someone holds. Moreover, the author maintains an attitude toward the reader and the thing that he is writing about which you must sense. For example, he may be dead serious and objective, such as when he writes a scientific article or chapter. Or he may be subjective and whimsical, such as when he writes about a personal experience. When you really comprehend a composition you understand both the author's purpose in writing and the attitude he maintains toward the reader and the things he is writing about.

The paragraph is the unit of organization within the composition. In giving structure to his composition the author organizes his paragraphs around some central scheme: comparing or contrasting; cause and effect relationships; analogy, for example. Part of your grasp of the whole composition depends upon your grasp of the principle that the author uses to bring order and organization to his individual paragraphs.

READING DIFFERENT KINDS OF MATERIALS

Although many reading skills are common to all materials

read, there are also many that are not. When you go into your mathematics classes, for example, you will be faced with reading demands that will not confront you in your English or chemistry or history classes. A large part of your success in your courses depends upon your success in meeting the demands placed upon you by the different materials of the content subjects.

The interpretation of data.

A considerable amount of information in science, mathematics, and social science is presented in forms of data. This means that you have the task of learning how to read tables, maps, charts and graphs with ease. Basic principles of reading data are the following:

Getting accurately the information presented in the data.

This includes knowing accurately terms that are used, reading arithmetic numbers accurately, using symbols correctly (legends, symbols representing mountains, contours, etc.) , understanding arithmetic terms commonly used in data—*average, area* for example.

Interpolating accurately.

This means going between points on the graph, chart or map to secure information. Included are relating information given on the base line to that given on the side line, making calculations, determining degrees or quantities, determining distances from a scale.

Extrapolating.

This refers to going beyond the information given in the data to form conclusions and make predictions.

Reading scientific and mathematical exposition.

Most scientific and mathematical prose requires slow, careful reading. Scientists and mathematicians pack information very closely into sentences and paragraphs. This means that you have to take plenty of time to dig it out. Moreover, you have the problem of extracting meaning from sentences containing both words, non-verbal symbols, and numbers: "the geometric mean of 3 and 12, for example, would be $\sqrt{(3)\ (12)} = \sqrt{36} = 6$." Or this example in physics, "Density is the mass of a body divided by its volume; that is, $D = M/V$." These examples show, also, that the reading of mathematics and science requires a thorough knowledge of symbols: $=$; $\div$; $\sqrt{}$; X; $(\ )$; $/$. Since science is based upon cause and effect relationships, reading of scientific materials requires you constantly to identify causes stated, and effects given, and to relate causes to effects, as in the following example: "Whenever energy is expended, force is exerted (cause). Force is the nature of a push or a pull (effect 1). Force is that which tends to change the condition of rest or motion of a body (effect 2)." Of course, it is evident that you need at all times an understanding of terms included in the passage.

Reading materials in the social studies.

Social sciences are made up of a number of individual fields: history, geography, economics, sociology, civics, anthropology. Each of these fields presents reading problems that are unique to it. In addition to a knowledge of the terms specific to each, all of them require special reading skills. History, for example, requires you to follow events in the order in which they are related, to associate dates with events, to determine characteristics of people and places, to determine causes and effects of wars and migrations, to form relationships between past events and present events. Geography demands that you learn topographical features, features concerning soil, climate, vegetation, land use, and so on. Economics demands that you read to learn about the production, distribution, and consumption of goods and services. Sociology subjects require you to master the origins, development, organization of human society. Each of the social sciences requires a "mind set" that is peculiar to it, and requires that if you are to succeed as a student that you must master the skills needed to read the different materials of these fields.

Reading in English and the Humanities.

In contrast to mathematics, science, and the social sciences which deal principally with fact, your reading in English and the Humanities most often takes you into the realm of imagination and emotion. Water may be H_2O (a material thing composed of 2 atoms of hydrogen combined with 1 atom of oxygen each with its own properties and weights, that produces 1 molecule of the substance we call water) to the scientist. A poet or writer is more concerned with a coloring of the imagination and stimulation of emotion when he writes of water as a babbling, gushing, sorrowful stream. Whereas the scientist uses terms and fact words the author uses metaphor and emotive words. Whereas the mathematician states proof the author creates a world of fancy inhabited by creatures of his imagination.

READING EXERCISES

Try out your abilities to comprehend by working out the four exercises below. They involve reading data, English, science and mathematics. Four passages are given, each followed by a number of statements. First, read the passage. Then read the statements. Decide in the light of information given in the passage whether each statement is *true* or *probably true,* or whether it is *false* or *probably false.* Then mark *T* (for true), *PT* (for probably true), *F* (for *false*), or *PF* (for *probably false*) in the parenthesis. In deciding upon answers you will have to read in different ways as have been explained in this section: grasp the literal or exact meaning; understand meaning suggested by words; interpret context; draw inferences; interpolate and extrapolate; understand terms. The correct answers are given in the appendix.

EXERCISE VIII

A. INTERPRETATION OF DATA

1. In 1920 the population of the South was 20 millions ... (   )
2. The population of the West grew at a faster rate than the populations of other sections of the country ...... (   )
3. Only the states above the Mason-Dixon Line are included in the term "North" .... (   )
4. In 1850 the population of the West was 200,000 .... (   )
5. Between 1850 and 1870 the West's population decreased (   )

6. A number of states bordering on the Atlantic Ocean are included in the term "North" .... (   )

7. The population of the West grew faster between 1890 and 1900 than between 1850 and 1860 .... (   )

8. The main purpose in the graph is to show how the populations of the whole country and its various parts changed between 1790 and 1940 .... (   )

9. The population figure for the United States in 1940 includes the 48 states, Alaska, Hawaii, and the Philippine Islands .... (   )

10. At some time between 1790 and 1940 the number of people living in the South equaled the number of people living in the North .... (   )

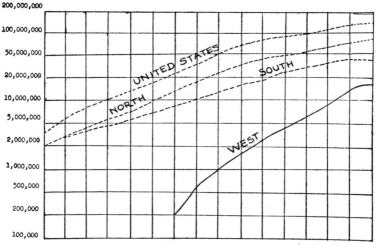

POPULATION OF THE UNITED STATES AND REGIONS: 1790 TO 1940

B. English

Lost

Desolate and lone
All night long on the lake
Where fog trails and mist creeps
The whistle of a boat
Calls and cries unendingly,
Like some lost child
In tears and trouble
Hunting the harbor's breast
And the harbor's eyes.
—*Carl Sandburg*

Statements

1. The tone of the poem is light and cheerful . . . . ( )
2. In speaking of the "harbor's breast" the author had in mind a part of the harbor called the breast . . . . ( )
3. The boat's whistle sounded long and moaning . . . . ( )
4. The "harbor's eyes" probably were the lights along the shore . . . . ( )
5. The boat blew its whistle because it felt lonely . . . . ( )
6. The crew of the boat was watching out for trouble . . . . ( )
7. The mist came up suddenly on the lake . . . . ( )
8. The boat behaved in the manner of a lost child . . . . ( )
9. The boat's whistle blew all night long in one continuous sound . . . . ( )
10. The fog streamed out over the lake . . . . ( )

C. Science

What Is A Lantern Slide?

In a negative we have the tones reversed. A negative is composed of a series of varying opacities. A white object such as the sky or a white dress is more or less dense or opaque, while a dark object or a deep shadow is more or less transparent. If a negative is examined by transmitted white light, the white dress is black and the dark object or deep shadow is white. We can make a print from a negative in which the tones are again reversed, this second reversal bringing them right. Such a print is a positive. We examine a print by reflected light, that is, the light falls on to the surface of the print and is thrown back or bent back. But if we make a print on glass or film using for the purpose a dry plate or a sensitive film, we still have a positive, but one which we must examine by looking through instead of at. Such a positive, because we can see through it, is often called a transparency. We examine it by transmitted light. Transparency, then, is a generic term for a positive picture on glass, or celluloid, or other transparent support. The support may even be of ground or opal glass, or the emulsion may have something added to it to give an opalescent or ground-glass effect, in which case it ceases to be transparent in the strict sense of the word, and is merely translucent, but it is still termed a transparency. Sometimes the expression "glass-positive" is used.

Such transparencies have various uses. They may be employed for window decoration, for lamp shades, for advertising purposes, and so on. They may be used for reproducing the original negative the same size, or larger or smaller. They may be made in small size and put into the projector or stereopticon and projected on to a white screen, in which case they are called lantern slides.

Statements

1. Black tones on the negative result from black tones on the objects photographed .... ( )
2. The negative lets light through in differing amounts .. ( )
3. When negatives are printed white objects photographed become black and black objects become white .... ( )
4. One main difference between positives and negatives is how each of them reacts to light .... ( )
5. The positive put on glass lets light through instead of bending it back .... ( )
6. Transparency is a term applied to positives put upon any types of materials that bend light back .... ( )
7. Supports made of ground glass have a milky color ..... ( )
8. Glass positives let as much light through as positives mounted on a dry plate or sensitive film .... ( )
9. Lantern slides are projected transparencies .... ( )

D. MATHEMATICS

Sum of the Angles of a Polygon

Draw a polygon of any number of sides. Let n stand for "any number." Draw all the diagonals from one vertex, (a diagonal is a straight line connecting any two non-adjacent vertices).

Notice that there are two fewer triangles than sides. Since there are n sides, there must be (n-2) triangles.

The sum of the angles of one triangle has been proved to equal 180°.

Hence the sum of the angles of (n-2) triangles is (n-2) —180°.

Statements

1. The drawn diagonals meet at one central point.
2. There are any number minus two triangles in a polygon having any number of sides.
3. We can draw the polygon having two sides.
4. Throughout the passage n means "any number."
5. The sum of the angles of a polygon (having any number of sides) is found by subtracting two from the number of sides and multiplying the results by one hundred and eighty degrees.
6. (n-2) is the number of angles in a polygon.

7. The author's main purpose is to show us how to find the sum of the angles in a polygon having any number of sides.

8. Diagonals can be drawn from the vertices of a triangle.

9. It is necessary to add in order to find a sum.

10. The polygon could have as many as fifty sides.

11. A polygon can have any shape.

12. The diagonal joins vertices located next to each other.

13. n is 3 when the expression $(n-2) \cdot 180°$ is applied to a triangle.

14. A diagonal is a line drawn from one vertex of the polygon to another vertex of the polygon.

Improving Writing Skills

A highly important part of the study and learning process is the ability to communicate ideas through writing. In our culture, one of the basic forms of communication is writing. When doing school assignments that are designed to improve this skill, the student is frequently required to submit evidences of his proficiency in the form of short, written daily reports, term papers, reading reports, or a research report, as it is called in colleges and universities.

In addition to the purpose of improving one's ability to communicate through the written word, the written assignment in school serves several other useful purposes in the student's total development. In the first place, it gives the student practice in using many of the study skills discussed in this book—in reading, note-taking, in using the library, in listening, and in general study and learning techniques. It also provides the student with an opportunity to apply the numerous principles, rules, and skills learned in his English courses. In many of the term reports assigned by the teacher, the student is required to use techniques and procedures that will help him become familiar with the independent study and research procedures that will constitute a large part of his study and learning in college and in other situations where he is left largely on his own. Through the collection of facts and materials required by the written report, the student also increases his *general* store of knowledge and acquires *specific* knowledge of a particular subject.

It is beyond the scope of this book to provide a complete discussion of grammar, rhetoric, and the many skills that make up "writing ability." It requires much time and effort in specialized learning situations to develop the ability to write effectively. These experiences will be provided in your English courses in school and by the practice you will get in writing reports assigned to you in your subjects. Increasing proficiency in writing will come as you progress in learning situations. The primary purpose of this section of the book is to give you some *practical guidelines* to be followed when you are doing written assignments. These guidelines are based on and summarize the principles concerning effective writing which you will learn in your many English courses.

Writing a good composition.

In discussing some guidelines for writing a good composition, the authors' aim is to provide you with some orderly steps of procedure that will result in a composition in which an idea or subject is *adequately treated* (explained) in a *logical coherent order* and in the kind of English that is acceptable, which is usually referred to as "standard" English. The guidelines given here are *not* concerned with the type of writing usually referred to as "creative writing"—the writing of stories, plays or poems. Instead, this discussion will deal with the type of writing referred to as *exposition composition*, which makes up a large part of all study and learning, regardless of the subject matter.

A composition should be thought of as a *process* involving several stages or steps. *Broadly* speaking, three identifiable steps involved are:

(1) *Pre-Planning* (consisting of several steps—selecting a subject, delimiting the subject, development of the *thesis* and developing an outline)
(2) *Rough Draft* ("fleshing out" the skeleton outline)
(3) *Revisions* (rewriting, changing, revising, improving)

Each of these three steps will be discussed below; however, one will see that the division between these three broad stages is not clear-cut.

PRE-PLANNING
The selection of a subject.

One basic process in the pre-planning stage is the *selection* of the topic (subject or idea) to be developed. It is obvious that before you can write a composition, you must know what you are going to write about. Many times, the topic for a composition is assigned by a teacher, or the topic will at least be partly determined by the wording of the assignment. For example, the assignment might request the student to write a composition dealing with some phase of space exploration. This assignment might suggest the topic "Some Effects of Weightlessness on the Human Organism." If you have a free choice in the selection of a topic, it is usually better to select one close to your interests and experiences; however, do not limit yourself to topics selected in this way, since one purpose of writing a composition (and doing the necessary research) is to provide you with *new* experiences and an opportunity to develop new *interests*.

Restricting (delimiting) the subject.

The matter of restricting the subject is as important as the selection of the topic. Once you have selected one from the several you might write about, the next step is to *refine* the topic in order to make it feasible for a composition; that is, the scope of the idea (topic) you choose to write about should not be so broad that you cannot treat (explain) it fully within a composition of reasonable length, such as is usually required in high school and college study.

The way to restrict your topic is to think of it not as a single experience but as a series of experiences. Restrict a topic that is initially too broad by breaking it down into sub-topics. In the illustration given above concerning the broad topic of Space Exploration, a sub-topic might be "The Effects of Weightlessness on the Human Organism," a further restriction might be a breakdown of the preceding topic into sub-sub-topics—"The Change in Pulse Rate During a State of Weightlessness," for example. The basic criterion to use in deciding how much the topic should be restricted depends on the *nature of the assignment*, if the topic has been assigned by the teacher. If the topic has not been assigned, the amount of restriction of the broad idea (subject) can be determined by asking and answering for yourself the following two questions:

(1) Can I rephrase the topic as a question?

(2) Can I answer this question *adequately* and *fully* in the space I am allowed (some assignments might call for a 500-word paper on a topic, other assignments might request a much longer paper).

If you have difficulty in rephrasing the topic as a simple question, try breaking it down into more sub-topics. The answer to the second question really sets the limit on the topic.

Statement of the thesis.

Another step in the pre-planning stage is known as "stating the thesis." As mentioned previously, the process of selecting a topic involved the restriction or the delimiting of an idea that was too broad to be treated in a single composition of reasonable length. The restricting of the idea was accomplished by selecting a sub-topic which is re-phrasable as a simple question. The *thesis* consists of the *answer* to the topic (or sub-topic) that you have rephrased as a question. Once you have phrased a question to be answered and once you have answered it carefully in *a single sentence,* you have the *thesis* of your composition.

The *thesis* is important for several reasons: It expresses clearly the idea to be explained; it puts a limit on the composition by suggesting what should be included and what should be left out; it serves as a guide to help you determine whether an idea being considered for inclusion is relevant or not (where there is a doubt, refer back to this *thesis*); and lastly, the *thesis* will help determine the organization (order) in which ideas and materials are to be presented. A good thesis is *unified* and *precise*. It states clearly the *single idea* the composition is to develop.

Developing the outline.

The last step in the pre-planning stage is the development of the outline for the composition. If you are writing a composition to tell the reader something then you must have a plan, or else he may get lost somewhere between the beginning and the end. The *plan* for a composition is embodied in its outline. The source of the outline is the *thesis* as was discussed above. The main topics you must cover in your composition come from a *careful analysis of the thesis*—dividing the thesis into its various parts. The following illustrations will help you see how to go about analyzing a thesis, which, in turn, will result in the *outline* (at least a tentative one) for the composition.

(1) Subject (before restricting):
   "Factors Affecting Personal Adjustment"

(2) Subject (restricted):
   "The Role of Habits and Attitudes in Personal Adjustment"

(3) Developing the thesis:
   (a) Question: How do habits and attitudes affect adjustment?
   (b) Answer (which is the *thesis*): "The successful unfolding of one's life is greatly influenced by the attitudes one holds and the habits one forms."

(4) Some topics suggested by the thesis:
   (i). The Meaning and Importance of Attitudes
   (ii). The Origins of Attitudes
   (iii). Attitudes Worth Developing
   (iv). The Modification of Attitudes
   (v). The Significance of Habits
   (vi). Kinds of Habits
   (vii). Characteristic of Habits
   (viii). Steps in Habit Formation
   (ix). Better Adjustment Through Habits and Attitudes
   (x). Etc.

After deciding on the *main* topics in the outline, the next step is to rephrase (in your mind) each of these topics as a question. The answers to these questions become sub-topics for the outline. This process is repeated until the thesis has been developed to your satisfaction; for example, in rephrasing topic iii above, you might ask: "What are the attitudes that are worth developing?" The answer might become several sub-topics, such as "respect for others," "independence," "industry," etc. Each of these sub-topics will be explained (discussed) in the writing of the composition.

WRITING THE COMPOSITION

The second broad stage in preparing the composition is the development of the outline by a discussion (explanation, elaboration) of each main topic and sub-topic in the outline. The first writing is known as a *rough draft*; it will later be revised and, hopefully, improved.

Sources of material.

A writer's materials are the data he uses to develop his thesis (or to carry out his purpose). These data may consist of facts, figures, ideas, beliefs, illustrations, case histories, quotations, comparisons, observations—anything he needs to develop his thesis. Despite the fact that "materials" are discussed under the section on the actual writing of the composition, this does not mean that materials are not needed in the pre-planning stages. In fact, materials play an important part in the selection of the subject, as well as in the development of the outline. Most of your materials will come from your experiences (reaction to stimuli which impinge upon your several sense organs) and from the interpretation or significance you give to these experiences. Some of these experiences come to you at firsthand, from your reactions to physical stimuli, while others are gained from reading. In school writing, many of your materials will come from your reading. For this reason, one should develop a high degree of reading skill, in addition to skill in locating pertinent material to be read in order to find the answers to the questions posed by the *thesis* in one's composition. Being able to read with understanding and to use the resources of a library efficiently are two of the basic skills needed for study and for learning.

Composing the materials (writing a paragraph).

Every composition you write must be a unit, regardless of

how long or short. All materials must be related to the *thesis*, and they must be placed in the logical order suggested by the outline. A composition is made up of paragraphs, and you must know the function of a paragraph when arranging your materials in a logical sequence. One writer has said that one should consider a paragraph as a miniature composition. It explains a *single* idea and explains it sufficiently—its parts "hang together." A paragraph has *unity, substance,* and *coherence.*

One way to guarantee unity in a paragraph is make sure that each paragraph has a *topic sentence.* This sentence is somewhat comparable to the function of the subject of the whole composition. Once you have the topic sentence, be sure that everything which follows in that paragraph is related to that sentence. Sentences not related to this topic sentence do not belong in that particular paragraph. Although many experienced writers might not include an *explicit* topic sentence; nevertheless, they define the paragraph by including only that which is relevant to an idea and excluding that which is not. A good idea for the beginning writer is to use the topic sentence as a guide to and as a control over what he is to include in and what he is to exclude from the paragraph.

The second element which must be considered in a paragraph is *substance*—the materials which go into the paragraph. These might consist of telling, explaining, describing, comparing, contrasting, showing cause and effect, listing details, examples, etc. To determine what substance (material) should go into a paragraph, do whatever is necessary to give the reader all that you want him to know about the *topic sentence.* It is also a good idea to check the *substance* of the paragraph by asking yourself "Is there anything here I can leave out and still have the reader know what he should about the topic sentence?"

The third element which characterizes the good paragraph is *coherence.* This means an arrangement of the materials (substance) in a logical order, or in a "natural" sequence, so that they hang together. If the paragraph has *coherence,* the reader can move easily from one sentence to the next, the second sentence must have some relation to the first, and so on. The reader must not feel that the sentences are unrelated, that something has been left out or that points have not been made. When the sentences are not related in this way, the reader feels that the sentence, not the paragraph, is the unit of writing. He will then read a series of separate statements instead of a discussion that is all related to a single idea. Paragraphs that lack coherence are the result of the writer thinking in single sentences rather than in a whole paragraph. Do not write one sentence, stop, think a minute, write another sentence and then continue in the same series of spurts and pauses. These pauses are likely to result in important details being left out, which makes for incoherence. Coherent writing can be achieved only from *much practice* of expressing one's ideas in writing.

Just as there must be coherence within a paragraph, there must also be coherence *between* paragraphs. If each topic sentence in each paragraph is related to the *thesis* of the composition, the relation between the paragraphs will be clear. The reader will be following the thesis; therefore, he should have little trouble seeing the relationship of each new paragraph to what has gone before. A good rule to remember in accomplishing unity *between* paragraphs is that the logic, the idea, and the facts must remain similar at the *end* of the preceding paragraph and at the *beginning* of the next. The identity of the idea is vital.

While it is beyond the scope of this book to teach grammar and logic, some of the following guidelines will help you improve your skill in composing and using the chief element of the paragraph—the *sentence*. If you recognize that you have a weakness in grammar and sentence structure, enroll in a class to get help or obtain an adequate handbook on grammar. Develop the ability to state your thoughts—not in random phrases or fragments, but in planned logical patterns and coherent, unified wholes. To state it simply, for writing to make good sense to the reader, the writer must first make good sentences. Everything in an effective sentence must relate to the purpose of the sentence as a whole; every word or punctuation mark used must contribute to the meaning of the sentence as a whole. In expository-type writing especially, *exclude* any material from the sentence which does not help the reader understand the thought you are trying to convey. Wordiness has its place in *creative* writing, but in expository writing, one should use no more words than are necessary to explain the idea fully.

Another characteristic of the good sentence is that the idea or sense of the sentence stands out or is emphasized. This might be accomplished in several ways—by choice of words, order or arrangement of words, repetition of key words, conciseness, and so on. Although effective sentences are characterized by conciseness, this does not mean that emphasis is to be sacrificed for conciseness. Avoid the monotony of too many similar sentences in succession—use variety. The beginning writer will, perhaps, be safest in making greater use of the simple or common sentence; however, he should aim at improving his knowledge and use of sentence structure to the point where he can employ a variety of sentence structures to convey his ideas. A good source of help in achieving variety in the use of words and phrases is *Roget's International Thesaurus of English Words and Phrases.* This volume is a rich source of suggestions for appropriate language. A copy can be found in your local library.

REVISING AND REWRITING THE COMPOSITION

The last part in the broad three-stage process of writing a composition (listed in the first part of this section) involves *revising* and *rewriting* the rough draft. For many writers, this phase of the process may require several revisions and rewritings (in whole or part) before they consider the composition satisfactory.

The purpose of the revision is to turn the rough draft into a finished composition. When revising, check to see that the composition conforms to the guidelines given in this section. Provide smooth transitions between units (topics and sub-topics) and polish diction (choice of words) and sentence structure to remove awkward constructions. Check to see that detailed information is related to the topic idea. Also check on the proper use of punctuation, misspelled or misused words, grammatical errors, and the like. These checks are more in the line of *proofreading*, while the former-mentioned items to be checked come under the heading of *editing*. Proofreading is aimed largely at identifying technical errors in the composition, while *editing* has for its purpose the improvement of the *quality* of the writing. A composition may be *technically correct* and still *poor in quality*. For the beginning writer, it is better to check each one of these suggested items throughout the whole composition, rather than attempting to make revisions in all these areas at the same time. Concentrating on one kind of error at a time is likely to yield better results. Careful and effective revision (editing and proofreading) of one's work requires much practice.

If you are enrolled in a class that is engaged in writing essays or compositions, it would be good practice to assume the role of critic when reading the papers of others. Organize cooperative-critic groups and exchange criticisms and suggestions for improvement. Do not take offense at unfavorable criticism. Usually, you will be able to pick up some clues which will be helpful to you in improving your writing.

In addition to the technical and quality aspects of the composition, its *appearance* is also important. There are no hard and fast rules when it comes to the format for a composition. Margins vary, titles are sometimes underlined, different systems of indention are used for paragraph beginnings, etc. In spite of a lack of uniformity, certain general principles are commonly applied. See the *suggested* format for a comparison as given below.

(1) The composition should be well balanced. The margins should be such as to provide a pleasing proportion of white space.

(2) Consistency of form is a must. If you start with an indentation of five spaces (or half an inch, if the writing is in longhand), continue to use the same indentation throughout. Establish appropriate margins for the first page, and use the same margins throughout. The top margin is the same throughout except for the first page, which contains the title.

(3) Neatness and legibility are important factors. Legibility is especially important if the composition is in longhand. It is better to type the composition if you have skill in the

use of a typewriter. Even when using a typewriter, try to type with a minimum of errors and erasures. A composition which looks carelessly prepared is not likely to receive the same degree of objective evaluation as one with a neat appearance.

(4) If the paper you are writing is an assignment, consult the teacher about any rules there might be for the format of your composition.

A suggested format for written reports (manuscripts).

The specifications given here will be helpful to students who are seeking a standardized form to follow in the preparation of written class reports and term papers. These are suggestions. Your teacher may have a specific format which he will want you to use; if so, follow his specifications. The important thing to remember is that the *form* of a report should never be emphasized at the expense of the *content* of the report. A good instructor will place more value on what you write than on the form or neatness of the report. However, the rules set down here will serve as a guide to help you concentrate on content, and you will not have to worry about both content and form if you use the suggestions given here. These rules apply to both handwritten and typewritten papers.

Written report form.

1. Paper: The manuscript should be typed double-spaced on unruled white paper, 8½" x 11" in size. (Ruled paper may be used if the manuscript is handwritten.)

2. Margins: All margins—top, bottom, and side—should be ample. The following margin dimensions are usually acceptable: 1½" at left, 1" at right, 1½" at the top, and 1" at the bottom. The margins you select (except for a greater top margin on the opening page) should be maintained throughout the paper. *Footnotes should not encroach on the margins.* The footnotes should be separate from the text. (See discussion on footnotes below.)

3. Numbering Pages: Pages should be numbered with arabic

numerals, usually placed in the upper-right hand corner. The first page of the manuscript need not be numbered.

4. Title: The title of the manuscript is usually typed on a separate sheet of paper. The title should also appear on the page on which the text begins, 2″ or 3″ from the top of the page.

5. Footnotes: Usually, the following rules apply: Footnote reference should run serially throughout the manuscript. If there are very few footnotes, a symbol or a sign (such as an asterisk) may be used. Otherwise, it is the practice to use superior (raised) numerals. (For a detailed discussion on rules for footnotes, consult a text on *thesis* or *manuscript writing.*)

A footnote should be separated from the text of the manuscript by a rule (line) approximately fifteen spaces long. In order to avoid crowding, a space is left above and below this line.

A number of abbreviations are used in footnote references. These can be found in the text mentioned previously.

6. Bibliography: On a separate page or pages at the end of the report, list the books, magazines, pamphlets, newspapers, and other sources of information you used in preparing your report. The list should be alphabetical by author. Where no author is listed, alphabetize by title, omitting articles *a*, *an*, and *the*. If you used many sources in preparing your report, books should be listed separately from magazine and newspaper articles.

In listing a book in your bibliography, include the author's *name, title, place, publisher,* and *date* of publication and the page numbers you are quoting. An example of how a book should be listed follows:

> Irving, Harris D. *Emotional Blocks to Learning* (New York: The Macmillan Company, 1961), pp. 42, 45.

In listing a magazine or newspaper article in the bibliography, include the author's name, the title of the article, the name of the magazine, the volume and number, date, and page numbers. A sample follows:

> Noble, C. E. "An Analysis of Meaning," *Psychological Review*, Vol. 59, Jan. 1952, pp. 421–430.

Before writing your report in the final form in which you will submit it to your instructor, check to see if the guidelines given above are acceptable.

Building Listening Skills

You learn in school through your *ears* as well as through your *eyes*. Experts who have studied human communication thoroughly have come up with some revealing facts. They show that the average individual spends approximately 70 per cent of his time communicating. Only about 9 per cent of this time is devoted to writing, 16 per cent to reading, 30 per cent to talking and *45 per cent* to listening. However, in spite of the large amount of time spent in listening the average person does not do it well. Estimates of listening efficiency show that the average skill is only about 25 per cent of what it should be.

You listen for many purposes and to satisfy many needs. You listen to radio programs for entertainment and information, to friends discuss their problems, to politicians seeking your vote, to members of the family, to salesmen trying to sell you some product. All of these require alertness and skills of many kinds. However, in school your main task is *listening to learn*. This requires that you listen to lectures in the classroom, directions in the laboratory, and speeches by prominent people. Your main objective is to secure facts and information through your ears. You can leave off listening for pleasure and entertainment until some more appropriate time.

LISTENING TO LECTURES

Preparing to listen.

You should know as much as you can about the speaker and his speech or lecture before you sit down to listen. If the speech is a classroom lecture the teacher may have provided you with a course outline or syllabus that will permit you to visualize beforehand what the subject of a specific lecture will be, and what will be included in it. You will then be prepared beforehand to expect what the main ideas will be, what details you can look for, and what the dimensions are (that is, the specific points where the speaker starts and stops). If the speaker is a chapel lecturer or assembly guest you should study the subject announced and visualize from it what he probably will cover. Also make a study of who the speaker is, his occupation, his title, and his expertness in his field. Such information will enable you to build up in your mind a framework into which you can fit the information provided by the speaker.

Acquiring a receptive attitude.

You don't just *assume* that you have a receptive attitude toward each lecture you listen to; often you have to build one. Many students allow their lack of interest in a subject to interfere with their grasp of materials presented orally. They lack maturity for becoming successful students because they cling to notions that learning must always be pleasant. Others permit their dislike of the teacher to disrupt their listening habits, or react emotionally to the lecturer's mannerisms or voice quality. Reason with yourself about why you are in school. Is it to like individuals, to be entertained, to be disturbed about the pecularities of people? Or is it to acquire the facts, information and skills that the school environment offers you in order that you can achieve the goals you have set for yourself? Look upon yourself during a lecture as taking part in a learning activity. Make up your mind that you will not permit your feelings to interfere with your learning.

Adjusting to the speaker.

Get into the habit of making a *conscious* effort to bring yourself in harmony with the speaker. Some speakers have loud, booming voices that you can hear well in any part of the room. Others speak more softly and you may have to sit nearby to hear them well. Speakers are human beings, so expect them to behave differently. Some pronounce every word and syllable with complete clarity. Others are not so articulate and you have to strain to understand them. Some speak with pleasing voice inflection. Others go along in a monotone. Since the speaker has what you want, it is up to you to adjust yourself to his delivery. Especially if the speaker is a lecturer whom you hear two or three times a week, is it necessary that you learn his ways of getting his ideas across.

An important aspect of listening consists of adjustment to the speaker's rate of delivery. When you read you can set your own rate. Moreover, if you have missed something you can go back on the page and re-read it. Once the word is spoken it may be gone for good. However, when you listen the speaker sets the rate. The rapid-fire speaker demands that you constantly stay on the alert to keep from missing important points. Especially if you take notes you must keep going at an accelerated pace. However much you must adjust to a speaker's rate there is no use in being a namby-pamby. Some classroom lecturers talk so fast that it is almost impossible to keep up with them and take useful notes at the same time. In such a case, speak up for yourself, and ask the lecturer to speak at a slower rate.

In contrast to the rapid-fire speaker is the slow, laborious lecturer. Although his speech may be more easily comprehended, his rate may be so slow that your mind has a chance to wander away between points he makes. In this case you may have to make a special effort to keep your attention on the alert.

Some speakers are precise, objective, and present clearly organized materials. It is much easier to adjust to this kind of speaker than the lecturer who often leaves his organized materials to insert witticisms or wise cracks. Frequently you have to adjust to lecturers who go beyond the presentation of facts and information to include personal experiences and irrelevant materials. In that you cannot prevent this you will have to bring yourself into harmony with the speaker's individuality as it exhibits itself.

Concentrating.

Avoid being a nervous listener. One important characteristic of listening is that it is *social*. You don't do it alone. Therefore you have to keep the behaviors of other people from distracting you. If you allow the rustling of paper or the scratching of a pen by your seatmate to draw your attention away from the speaker you stand to miss important information. If your ears are attuned to a cough rather than to the speaker you can get off the track. Or if the new hair-do of the girl sitting in front of you keeps drawing your attention you are not listening as you should. Such distractions are the result on your part of habit, or impatience, or lack of will power. If you are easily distracted you will need to establish new and more effective habits.

The great enemy to concentration is the habit of day-dreaming. People day-dream because they live too much in a world of their own imagining, or they wish to escape reality, or they lose interest in present proceedings. Day-dreaming is all right when you have nothing else to do, but it has no place in listening to a speaker. Many students day-dream because they are not conscious of the fact that they have the habit. When they do realize it they can break the habit by recognizing when they do go off into day-dreams, and pulling themselves sharply out of it. By constantly practicing they finally learn to master the habit. Some students allow the way a speaker is dressed, or the way he stands, or his gestures with his hands to distract them. Again there are habits which you must break if you have them. Breaking a habit, however, is not enough. You must replace the old habit with a new one. Deliberately keeping attention on the speaker's face, for example, might correct the habit of letting your attention wander to the speaker's clothes or his mannerism of folding his hands after he makes a point.

Getting the speaker's message.

Fortunately lecturers in school take time to organize their speeches. The informative speech is divided into four recognizable parts. First comes the *introduction,* second the *proposition* the speaker will defend or expound upon, third *the body of the* speech, and fourth the *conclusion.* You listen to the introduction to determine how the speaker "sets up" his speech. He seeks in it to establish a meeting place with the audience, to command attention, to stimulate interest. The speaker may do this by telling an anecdote or describing some situation known both to him and his listeners. Frequently a classroom lecturer will use his introduction to form connections in your mind between preceding lectures and the present one. If you are an alert listener you may use the introduction to study the style and delivery of the speaker and to decide upon what steps you must take to adjust yourself to him.

When he finishes his introduction the speaker shifts to his proposition and you shift with him. Now is the time to listen intently, because he sets before you the idea, fact or belief to which he has committed himself. Be on the lookout for expressions such as "Our concern today is with ———"; "I shall speak to you about ———"; "What are the main causes of ———?" The speaker is signaling to you that he has finished with his introduction and is placing his "big idea" before you. Also listen for other words that the speaker may use to help you follow the development of his "big idea." He may say, for example, that the first part of his speech will deal with some specific aspect of it, the second part will deal with another aspect, and the third part will conclude and summarize. The speaker is doing his best to help you get his message, so use his help.

The speaker develops his proposition or "big idea" in the body of the speech. He chooses main points that bear out the proposition. Your task as listener is to get a firm grasp of the main points and see clearly how they support the "big idea." There are only a few main points in most speeches but they contain the gist you are after. Usually when the speaker leaves one main point to go on to another he signals through a transitional expression that he is shifting. Be on the lookout for expressions such as "Let us move on to ———"; "Turning now to ———"; "Next in order ———." Such transitional expressions not only provide a bridge for helping you move logically from one part to another. They also warn you to be on the alert to grasp the next main point.

The speaker further supports main points with sub-points. The main point is a general statement. The sub-points are specific. They may lend support by illustrating, by presenting details of how a thing looks or acts, by comparing and contrasting, or stating cause and effect.

The final part of the speech is the conclusion. It is usually brief. You listen for several things. First of all, the speaker signals when he is concluding by using expression such as "Finally ———"; "In conclusion ———"; "In summary ———." Second, you listen for a re-statement of the main points in concise form which helps to "fix" them in your mind. The speaker may attempt, also, to apply what he said by suggesting how people or living conditions may be improved by what he has said. A classroom lecturer might tell you in his conclusion how the information given you fits in with the scope of the course or relate it to a specific assignment.

Filtering the speech.

Even before you begin to listen to a speaker you recognize the fact that everything he says cannot possibly have value for you. Neither can you expect to retain each word, each phrase, each item of information as a tape recorder might do. Therefore you select and reject according to a reasoned plan.

Keep before you that the "meat" of the speech is presented in the main points. Always select and retain all of them. Since there are not many, you will not find this too difficult. However, it is useless to retain all the sub-points the speaker may use to support the main points. Two or three from a larger number will most often do the trick. For example, under the main point below sub-points 1, 2, and 3 give the important *sense* and the others can be ignored:

Main point: Communication is a big thing in the United States today

Sub-point 1: Radio programs reach practically every home
(Retain)   throughout the country

Sub-point 2: Hundreds of millions of dollars are invested in
(Retain)   the television industry

Sub-point 3: Americans have more telephones per family than
(Retain)   any country in the world

Sub-point 4: "Talking" records may be found now in most
(Forget it) music stores.

Sub-point 5: Disc jockeys are increasing in number
(Forget it)

When you listen, you listen *critically* and *alertly* in order
that you can constantly separate the chaff from the wheat.

It is too much to expect every speaker to be perfectly logical
so that his sub-points *always* support main points. Frequently
you will hear sub-points that go off on a tangent. You are
thinking with the speaker as he *thinks*. You relate his ideas to
things in your experience. When you make connections between
the two you get *meaning*. If your experience is too limited to
react to the author his speech is meaningless or you may mis-
interpret it. When he gets off the point simply ignore his di-
gression and wait until he gets back on the track. However, be
on the lookout for signals such as "Incidentally ———"; "In
addition to ———"; "Supplementary to ———." The speaker
is indicating that he is supplying information additional to that
already given to develop a main point.

Restraining emotion.

Listening to an informational speech requires you to keep
your emotions under control. We know that people tend to
"read too much" into printed materials. They allow their own
feelings, convictions and biases to color the information gained
from the page. It is possible to "listen too much" into a speech
that you hear. You can permit unthinkingly your own notions,
feelings, and prejudices to distort a speaker's information. Keep
the purpose always before you that you listen to an informational speech to *get information accurately*. After you have got
it *accurately* you can decide whether you want to take it "lying
down," or whether it goes against your convictions. But, first,
get the message!

Following directions.

In school activities such as laboratory work and military
science you constantly receive oral directions. For example, the
science teacher might give you directions about setting up a
piece of laboratory equipment, or a squad commander may tell

you how to go about executing a military formation. In either case your success depends upon the accuracy with which you have listened to and understood directions.

Listening to directions demands that you grasp a series of activities in chronological order. You are told what comes first, second, and so on, and you must establish through your ears the *order* of activity. You will get things all mixed up if you substitute activity 4 for activity 3, or 2 for 5. In cases where there are only a few activities required of you and none are complicated grasping them in order is not difficult. In cases where activities are complex and numerous you should check your oral understanding by writing each down in the order in which it occurs, and checking the sequence against the original. Do not hesitate to ask an instructor to repeat his directions if your grasp of the order of activities is uncertain.

Following directions also demands an accurate knowledge of terms used by the "director." For example, if setting up equipment in the laboratory requires you to use a thistle-tube and you do not know what it is, you can accomplish very little. Or if you are told to draw lines on the blackboard from a vertex you will have to know what *vertex* means before you can carry out the directions. You should see that you know accurately the meanings of all terms before you attempt to carry out the directions.

Following directions also demands a grasp of limitations either stated or implied. You cannot "over-do" nor "under-do" what you are told and be accurate. You listen closely to the directions to determine in reality what you are permitted to do and what you are not permitted to do. The story of the sergeant who commanded his men to march and turned aside to get a cinder out of his eye, has a point. When he next looked up his men were disappearing over a cliff because he had not commanded them to halt. Effective listening, then, requires that you attain skill in preparing for what you will hear, forming an objective and receptive attitude toward the speaker, concentrating on the ideas presented by the speaker, interpreting these ideas, and selecting those ideas which will complete your learning experience.

EXERCISE IX

Select a scheduled speech or lecture at your school or in your community (or one assigned by your teacher) and complete the following exercises:

A. Prior to the speech or lecture, ascertain the speaker's subject and make a list of the points you anticipate that the speaker will cover in his message (try to visualize the things the speaker will say)

B. After listening to the speech or lecture, identify the following parts of the speaker's message:

    (1) Introduction— (a) How did he introduce his speech?

                    (b) Try to quote one of his introductory statements.

    (2) Proposition— (a) Specifically, what was the central idea of the speech?

                    (b) List several of the *main* points related to this central idea.

    (3) Conclusion— (a) How did the speaker signal that he was bringing his speech to a close?

C. What parts of the speech could the speaker have omitted without doing harm to the central idea of his speech?

D. What parts of the speech had little meaning for you? Why did these parts have less meaning for you than did other parts of his speech?

E. What mannerisms, if any, did the speaker have which tended to distract you? How may one overcome such distractions?

HOW TO CLEAR THE EXAM HURDLES!

Developing Examination Skills

Examinations (tests and quizzes) occupy an important place in all school and college programs. It is important that you develop the proper attitude toward them, and acquire a "know how" that will enable you to work at top efficiency when taking them. There is nothing in this section that will tell you how to pass an examination if you have not learned the materials beforehand. However, you will be given suggestions on how to use effectively what you have learned, when faced with an examination. Since the purpose of examinations is to measure how effectively you have learned, the basic preparation for them is a thorough mastery of the subject matter prior to taking the examination. The materials presented in the other sections of this book will help you to acquire this mastery. However, it is known that many students either fail examinations or make low scores *not* because they have failed to master the subject matter, but because they have not acquired skill in effectively using their knowledge to answer examination questions. Also, many students do poorly on examinations because they have developed unwholesome attitudes toward them. In the same manner that a lack of skill in answering examination questions will adversely affect your performance on examinations, a negative attitude toward them will also reduce your efficiency. You have a negative attitude when you view an examination as a means your teacher uses to "trip you up" rather than view it as an opportunity to check on how effectively you have learned.

Many students have a negative attitude toward examinations, perhaps, because they have not inquired into the true purpose of examinations. Some of the basic purposes are the following:

Examinations indicate the progress of both the student and the teacher.

When your teacher examines the answers you write to examination questions, he is able to see what you have or have not learned. This knowledge can be of help to him in planning future learning activities for his class. A careful study of your examination paper after it has been corrected by the teacher can be of vital help to you. You will have a better idea of your strengths and weaknesses--things which have been learned well, and things which need to be relearned. This knowledge can serve as a guide in your future study activities. Your deficiencies, as revealed by the examination, may indicate that you need to spend more time in study, change your method of study, or take special courses to increase your knowledge and understanding.

Examinations encourage effective study.

Frequent examinations usually will cause students to engage in more serious study than they would do otherwise. Teachers have observed that students are likely to engage in regular, consistent daily study when they know that a quiz or examination may come without warning. Many teachers give unannounced quizzes.

Examinations serve as a basis for grades.

Whether you like them or not, grades are still used to indicate how well or how poorly you have learned. It is important that you begin on the first day of school to build a good record, including grades.

Examinations are important in life after school.

In addition to measuring how well you have learned in school, examinations play an important role in your life after you leave school. You are likely to be faced with examinations of one kind or another for the rest of your life. You will, no doubt, be required to take an examination to demonstrate your fitness for a job. Also, your advancement or promotion on your job is likely to depend, at least in part, on the results of an examination.

TYPES OF EXAMINATIONS

The examinations you will take in school are likely to be either the *essay* or *objective* (sometimes called short-answer) type. Examinations are usually classified on the basis of the type of question used. The more technical term for a test question is "test item." Hereafter, this term, test item, will be used instead of test question.

The essay examination.

This type requires you to *recall* the subject matter you have learned, and to *organize* it in such a way to form a logical answer to the question asked on the examination. The essay examination not only measures your ability to recall subject matter, but may require you to *interpret* it or to *apply* it in some new situation. This type of examination measures your ability to organize your thinking about a topic or idea, and then to present your thoughts in clear and logical form. It will require you to do more writing than the objective type. Items used on the essay examination usually begin with such words as Discuss, Explain, Compare, Describe, List, and Indicate. The following are typical of items found on the essay examination:

—Describe a good study environment

—List three factors essential to success with school work

The objective examination (short-answer type).

The objective examination is one that requires a minimum of writing. Answering items usually requires the insertion of a single word or brief phrase in a space provided, or inserting a symbol of some kind to indicate your choice of the correct or best answer from among several possible answers provided. The types of objective questions or items commonly used in school work are: (1) *alternate-response* item, (2) *multiple-choice* item, (3) *completion* item, and (4) *matching* item.

Alternate-response item.

In this type, two alternatives (true-false, yes-no, right-wrong, correct-incorrect, etc.) are presented along with a statement. After reading the statement, the student is to select *one* of the two alternatives as being correct for the statement. The two items below are examples of this type.

(—) Listening to soft music while studying helps one to concentrate

(—) Studying while relaxed on a couch aids concentration

In the above examples, a plus sign (+) is used for a true statement; a minus sign (—) for a false statement. Since both statements are false, a minus sign has been placed in the parenthesis before each of them.

Multiple-choice item.

The multiple-choice item consists of two parts: Part I presents a statement of the problem, which may take the form of a question or incomplete statement; Part II presents a series of suggested answers (3-5 possible answers are usually provided) of which only one is correct or best. The task of the person taking the examination is to pick this correct or best answer. The two items below are typical of this type.

(3) The best temperature for study is approximately (?) °F.

(1) —80° (2) —75° (3) —68° (4) —50° (5) —85°

(3) If you spend 15 hours per week in class, you should study a minimum of (?) hours per week.

(1) —18 (2) —25 (3) —30 (4) —5 (5) —20

In the examples above, the person taking the examination is required to place the *number* of the correct answer in the parenthesis before the statement. The correct answers are given.

Completion item.

The completion type item usually takes the form of a statement with certain important or essential words missing. The student taking the test is to supply the missing information. Two examples of this type item are given below.

(10) If a student has a job which requires him to work 6 hours per day, he should not pursue more than _____ semester hours of school work.

Four types of objective test items are 1 *(multiple-response)*

2 *(alternate-response)*

3 *(completion)*

4 *(matching)*

Matching item.

The simplest form of the matching test item consists of two columns of words or phrases to be matched on some basis indicated in the directions. Each word or phrase in one column is related to a word or phrase in the other column in some specified way. The person taking the test is required to select the number of the word or phrase in one column that matches a word or phrase in the other column. For example, the left hand column may contain the names of inventors; the column on the right might contain the names of their inventions, arranged in random order. The task, in this case, is to match the names of inventors with the names of their inventions. This kind of item is used in the matching of such materials as events and dates, events and places, events and results, books and authors, usages and rules, products and processes. Examples are given below.

OPERAS	COMPOSERS
(7) Faust	1. Jules Massenet
____	2. Giuseppe Verdi
(4) Carmen	3. Giacomo Puccini
____	4. Georges Bizet
(6) William Tell	5. Gaetano Donizetti
____	6. Gioacchino Rossini
(2) Aida	7. Charles Gounod
____	

In the above example, you are required to place in the space proceding each opera on the left the *number* of the composer from the column on the right. More composers than operas are listed to reduce the chances of matching by guessing. In the example below, the task is to match roots and meanings.

Root		Meaning
(3)	acer	1. walk
(2)	amare	2. love
(4)	aer	3. sharp
(1)	ambulare	4. air
(5)	brevis	5. short
		6. strong
		7. sleep

Standardized examination.

Another examination form employing the objective type item is the *standardized* examination. It differs from the objective examination constructed by the classroom teacher in two respects. It is usually more refined than those made by the teacher; that is, it has been tried out on many persons, and has been through several stages of revisions before it is printed and published. Also it has a wider use. The standardized examination can be given to students throughout the country and their performances can be compared. In addition to the measurement of school learning, the standardized examinations are used to measure such factors as intelligence, personality, attitudes, and interests. The teacher-made test deals primarily with the measurement of achievement.

PREPARING FOR EXAMINATIONS

The best preparation you can make for an examination is to engage in regular and consistent daily study. However, the following suggestions will enable you effectively to use the subject matter you have learned when you are faced with an examination.

Develop wholesome attitudes.

Consider examinations as a means of increasing the effectiveness of your learning, rather than as another necessary evil.

WILL YOU LOOK LIKE THIS
AT EXAM TIME?

Such an attitude is likely to prevent you from working at top efficiency when taking an examination, and will result in your earning a low or failing score. Negative attitudes increase the likelihood of your making many needless errors while taking an examination.

Maintain good health.

Mind and body work together. A poor physical condition will lower your mental efficiency. In preparing for an examination, observe the common-sense rules of health. Get sufficient sleep and rest, eat proper foods, plan recreation and exercise. In relation to health and examinations, two cautions are in order. Don't miss your meals prior to an examination in order to get extra time for study. Likewise, don't miss your regular sleep by sitting up late to "cram" for the examination. Cramming is an attempt to learn in a very short period of time what should have been learned through regular and consistent study spread over the entire semester. Not only are these two habits detrimental to health, but seldom do they pay off in terms of effective learning. It is likely that you will be *more confused* than better prepared on the day of the examination if you have broken into your daily routine by missing your meals or sleep.

Engage in regular and consistent study.

The time to begin preparation for an examination is on the very first day of the class. Most school learning is acquired by spreading your learning efforts over a reasonable period of time. Things learned in a hurry are seldom completely learned, and are soon forgotten. Don't attempt to crowd into a day or two the learning that should have been spread over the entire semester. If you will prepare your assignments daily, review regularly and selectively, you will have no need to "cram" for an examination.

Review your notes regularly.

Observe the principles of notetaking as discussed in Section VI of this book. After taking effective notes on your learning experiences—in and out of class—review these notes regularly.

A brief daily review of your notes along with a more intense review once a week will be required if they are to be of maximum use to you. In reviewing your notes, give special attention to those relating to topics on which the teacher spent a great deal of time. It is likely that these topics are considered of sufficient importance to be included in the quiz or examination. Some of the important materials in any course, and the ones likely to be included in the examination are *vocabulary* (special terms used in class or found in your reading) , *formulas, laws,* and *principles.* Whenever you come across such materials, be sure that they get into your notes and are marked in such a manner that your attention will be called to them during your reviews.

Hold "bull" sessions.

Have study sessions with other students who have reasonably mastered the subject matter. Fire questions back and forth. Practice phrasing your answers as you would on the examination in the subject. If questions arise which no one in the group can answer, go back and review or relearn this material. See earlier discussion in this book dealing with group study.

Review previously written assignments.

As soon as your teacher corrects and returns your written assignments, including examinations, go over your papers to see where you made your mistakes. Make it a policy to correct these mistakes the same day your papers are returned to you. Prior to an examination, review all of your previously written assignments.

Study the examinations given previously in a class.

Many schools follow the practice of placing on file in the library or in some other convenient location copies of all examinations which have been given previously in the class. If these old copies are available, carefully examine them. They can give you some idea of the nature of the subject matter likely to be included in the examination, its scope, and type of test items likely to be employed. While a review of these old examination copies can be useful as guides in preparing for your examination, by no means confine your study to the subject matter included in them. Try to identify the important materials in a course and learn them regardless of whether these materials have been included on previous examinations in the course.

Develop poise and self confidence.

Develop an ability to "loosen up" when taking examinations or when engaging in any task that requires concentration. An *excess* amount of tenseness and anxiety tends to hinder concentration. Report to the examination place in a calm and relaxed state. There is no need to caution you against being too relaxed. The concern created by the examination is usually enough to prevent this. The ability to relax results largely from having confidence in yourself. Self-confidence can be developed by "knowing your stuff" at examination time. Usually confidence in one's self is lowered when one realizes that he is not able to cope with a situation that confronts him. A lack of self-confidence during an examination usually results when your learning has been so "spotty" that you are not sure of any of your information or knowledge. After you have done your best to master the subject matter by engaging in regular and consistent study, look upon an examination as a competitive game —win if you can, lose if you must, but do the best you can. Excessive worry or anxiety over the examination will prevent you from effectively using the knowledge that you do have.

TAKING EXAMINATIONS

In addition to establishing effective habits in preparing for examinations, it is also important that certain basic principles govern your behavior during the examination period. The following suggestions will enable you to make the most effective use of your previous preparation. Make a mental check list of these suggestions and check your behaviors against them during your next examination.

Be on time.

Go to the examination room in time to get settled before the examination begins. A good rule is to arrive at the appointed place at least five minutes before the examination is scheduled to start. Allowing yourself ample time avoids the danger of emotional upset which can result from last minute rushing. The usual practice in testing is not to allow anyone to enter the testing room after the time scheduled for the test to begin. This is done to avoid the distraction caused by late-comers, and also to be sure that everyone hears all of the directions necessary for the test. The teacher or test supervisor usually begins to read these directions promptly at the time the test is scheduled to start.

Bring all necessary equipment.

Take to the examination room everything that will be necessary in taking the examination—pen, pencils, paper, eraser, or other materials as might be designated in the directions you receive before reporting for the test. If an ordinary pencil is to be used, it is well to have two or more sharpened ones in your possession. This will avoid delay or waste of valuable time should the point break.

Get settled.

Find your seat in the examination room and stay in it. If no special seats have been assigned, occupy a seat near the front of the room. This facilitates the seating of other persons coming in after you. If you talk with your neighbor before the examination begins, do so in subdued tones. Await quietly the instructions for the examination. If you are taking a standardized examination, there will be, perhaps, a test supervisor and test proctors in the room. The person who reads the directions for the test and otherwise tells you what to do is the *test supervisor.* The persons who walk about the room passing out examination materials and otherwise assisting with the examination are *test proctors.* If after finding your seat you are not able to see or hear properly, notify the test supervisor or a proctor. Likewise, if you have other difficulty during the examination, raise your hand to command the attention of one of the proctors. When he reports to your seat, inform him of your difficulty. These difficulties might involve such things as having a defective pencil, test booklet, or answer sheet. If such is the case, it is the job of the proctor to replace it with a good one.

Relax.

Don't bring on unnecessary worry or anxiety by trying to anticipate the difficulty of the examination. Make yourself wait a minute or two before you begin to write. If you still feel tense, take several deep breaths, check your test equipment—paper, pencil, test booklet, or engage in some other activity at your seat which will temporarily take your mind away from the examination. Some of this tenseness will, perhaps, leave you once you begin to write the examination. However, the best guarantee against such anxiety is to "know your stuff" when you report for the examination. This can be accomplished through daily study and review prior to the examination.

Understand the directions.

If the directions for the examination are written, read them carefully, at least twice. If the directions are given orally, listen attentively and then follow them precisely. For example, if the directions indicate that you are to use plus (+) and minus (—) to indicate true or false items, then don't use "T" and "F." If the directions instruct you to "blacken" a space as on machine scored tests, do not use an "X." Make all symbols legible, and be sure that they have been placed in the proper answer space. It is easy, for example, to place the answer for item 5 in space reserved for item 6. If this is done, then all of your following answers may be wrong. It is also very important that you understand the method that will be used in scoring the examination if it is included in the directions. The method of scoring may affect the amount of time you spend on an item, especially if some items will count more than others. Likewise, the directions may indicate whether or not you should guess in case you are not sure of the answer. Some methods of scoring will penalize you for guessing. If you don't understand the directions you have heard or read, raise your hand and inform the teacher or proctor. If the test has more than one part, read carefully the directions for each part before beginning to work on that part. If you skip over such directions too hastily, you may miss a main idea and thus lose credit for an entire section.

Get an overview of the examination.

After reading the directions carefully, look over the entire examination to get an overview of the nature and scope of the test. Especially scan the *entire* examination if it is a short teacher-made (or classroom) quiz or test. On standardized examinations you are allowed to examine *only* the section of the examination that the supervisor has announced—you can't, for example, examine the questions in Part II of an examination until the time allowed for Part I has expired and you have been instructed to begin Part II. The purpose of this overview is to give you some idea of the nature, scope, and difficulty of the examination. It has another advantage. Certain of the essay items may contain clues or stimulus words that will help you arrive at the answer to some of the other items. By stimulus words is meant those words which at the sight of them alone brings certain ideas to your mind that might not have come otherwise. In the sample essay items on page 142 for example, the term "over-learning" in item 5 might be sufficient to cause you to recall the class discussion on the importance of review. If so, then your having read over all the questions would have been helpful in answering item 5 or item 7 which deal with the importance of review. Likewise, an item might be so phrased that it sets in motion a chain of thought that might be helpful in answering other items on the examination. Still another benefit to be derived from reading all the items before you answer any is that the minute or two involved in reading the items gives you an opportunity to relax or to compose yourself before beginning the examination. This will make for better concentration. As you read over these items the first time, check those whose answers come immediately to you. These will be the ones you will answer first. Read each item carefully before answering. It is a good practice to read each item at least twice to be sure that you understand it.

Work rapidly but carefully.

Once you start to write the examination, follow the rule—

work as rapidly as you can, but as carefully as you can. If you come to an item whose answer does not immediately come to you, skip that one and come back to it later.

Avoid fatigue.

If the examination is overly long (two hours or more) give yourself a rest period, even if a very shoit one. If you are not permitted to leave the room, relax in your seat and close your eyes for a minute or two. These rest pauses help to keep your mental efficiency at a high level. Rest periods are usually provided during standardized tests if they are of long duration.

Edit your paper.

Before submitting your paper, look it over to check spelling and punctuation. Also, save some time to check your paper for any changes that you may need to make in your answers. This applies especially to essay-type examinations.

To guess or not to guess on objective examinations.

Read the directions carefully to determine the scoring method that will be used. In some tests, the directions will indicate that guessing is advisable if you do not know the answer to a question. In such tests, only the right answers are counted in determining your score. If such is the case, don't omit any items. If you do not know the answer, or if you are not sure of your answer, then *guess*. On the other hand, if the directions state that a scoring formula *will* be used in determining your score or that you are *not to guess*, then *omit* the question if you do not know the answer, or if you are not sure of the answer. When the scoring formula is used, a percentage of the *wrong* answers will be subtracted from the number of *right* answers as a correction for haphazard guessing. It is improbable, therefore, that mere guessing will improve your score significantly. *It may even lower your score.* Another disadvantage in guessing under such circumstances is that it consumes valuable time that you might profitably use in answering the questions you know. If, however, you are not sure of the correct answer but have *some* knowledge of the question and are able to eliminate one or more of the answer choices as wrong, your chance of getting the right answer is improved, and it will be to your advantage to *answer* such a question rather than *omit* it.

Using the special pencil.

If you are taking an examination which requires the use of a special pencil (usually a #2 graphite pencil) be sure to *use that pencil only*. These pencils are used when the test is to be scored by a machine. If you use an ordinary pencil, the machine will not record your answer. If you have an occasion to erase an answer on such tests, *do so completely*. If you do not do a good job of erasing, the machine will record the answer you attempted to erase. Likewise do not make any stray marks on your answer sheet with these special pencils. Such marks may be recorded as wrong answers by the machine. When you are not writing, remove the special pencil completely away from the answer sheet to avoid accidentally making stray marks. It is also important that you hold this special pencil firmly in order to make a *heavy* and *distinct* mark.

ANSWERING EXAMINATION ITEMS

The suggestions below are designed to help you make a more effective approach to the answering of certain types of test items. While there is no way to avoid the necessity of knowing the subject matter covered by the test, there are effective and non-effective ways of using your learning to answer test items. The essay, alternate-response, multiple-choice, completion, and matching type test items will be discussed. First you will be given some sample items for the several types, then there will follow suggestions for answering each type of examination item.

HOW TO ANSWER THE ESSAY EXAMINATION ITEM [1]

—Some sample essay items

    1. *Compare* standardized and teacher-made tests in respect to use in the classroom.

---

[1] While the sample essay examination items in this section are used for illustrative purposes, use them as exercises to check on your understanding of the materials in this book.

2. *Explain* the concept of retroactive inhibition.
3. *Summarize* the advantages and limitations of a study schedule.
4. *Criticize* the statement—"One should study at least two hours for every hour spent in class."
5. *Evaluate* the concept of "over-learning" as a sound study procedure.
6. *Name* three factors that are basic to school success.
7. *Discuss* the place of review in learning.
8. *Outline* the principal steps in preparing an assignment.
9. *List* five suggestions that are applicable to *preparing* for examinations. *Taking* examinations.
10. *Define* the word "cramming."

Locate key words in the item.

Each essay item has a key word, stated or implied. These key words have an instructional value in that they tell you what to do in answering the item. Some examples of such key words are compare, discuss, evaluate, explain, enumerate, contrast, describe, define, criticize, diagram, summarize, review, relate, illustrate, interpret, outline, prove, list, and justify. In the sample essay items given above, each key word has been italicized. Find key words and be guided by them. If the key word in an essay item is *list,* for example, your answer should consist of a *series* of things *itemized.* This series of statements should be concise and to the point. If the key word is *evaluate,* then your answer should cite advantages and disadvantages of the thing being discussed. If the key word is *summarize,* then give the *main* points or facts in a *concise* form, omitting minor detail. Each key word should be analyzed in this manner to determine *specifically* what you are to do in answering the item. A key word in an item might be implied rather than explicitly stated. For example, an essay item might require you to evaluate something. However, the word *evaluate* might never appear in the item. The following essay item is such a case: "What kind of examination provides the best measurement of one's ability to organize and express his thoughts?" Although this item will require you to make an evaluation of many different kinds of examinations, the word evaluate does not appear in the item, Key words are important. Look for them.

Think and organize.

After you have read the item at least twice, organize your answer mentally *before* you begin to write the answer. During this period in which you are thinking about the answer, try to recall the relevant things you have read in the your textbook, heard in class or performed as experiments in the laboratory. After you have recalled the materials necessary for answering the item, organize your answer mentally. A good procedure in organizing your answer is to list on a piece of scrap paper the essential points you wish to discuss in your answer. Your notations on this piece of scrap paper will take the form of a one or two-word outline. To conserve time, you may even use abbreviations. The important thing is to list points in some manner so that you will not forget them when you begin to write. For example, in answering the essay item—"Discuss some factors important in the preparation for examinations" your brief outline may contain such reminders as attitudes, daily study, weekly review, old exams, health, etc.

Be concise.

Remember that the *quality* of what you write and not how much you write is the important thing in writing an essay answer. A concise answer leaves a favorable impression on the teacher. It indicates that you clearly understand the materials you are discussing. In being concise, however, be sure that you write enough to indicate that you know the answer. Don't leave too much to be inferred. If the item is of such a nature as to require a lengthy answer, use a summarizing statement at the beginning. That is, write the gist of the answer in the first sentence, then elaborate in the following sentences.

Don't bluff.

If you can only partly answer an item, then write as much as you know. Do not attempt to add to your answer by writing a lot of statements unrelated or only partly related to the item. Teachers are quick to spot such bluffing or "padding" as it is sometimes called. When they once spot such an answer, they are likely to read your paper with much more scrutiny than they would have done otherwise.

Illustrate.

Strengthen your answers wherever possible through the use of illustrations. Cite examples, draw charts, make use of diagrams, wherever such will help to clarify your answer. When using sketches in your answers, do not attempt to make them art masterpieces. This will consume too much time. The ability to illustrate your answer indicates a thorough understanding of the materials.

Express your thoughts correctly and effectively.

In writing your answers to essay items, observe accepted rules relating to grammar and effectiveness of expression. Observe rules of spelling, punctuation, sentence structure, etc. You may have sufficient knowledge to answer an essay item, but because of errors in spelling and punctuation, or poor sentence structure, the teacher will never discover what you are attempting to say.

Be legible and neat.

Be sure that your answers are legibly written, and that your paper has a neat appearance. Don't crowd your words or sentences. Leave enough space between your answers so that the teacher will know where one stops and another begins. Leave a margin on both sides of the paper. Unless otherwise instructed, write only on one side of the page.

Number your answers correctly.

Be sure that the numbering of your answers corresponds to the numbering of the items on the examination. This becomes especially important when you do not answer the items in the same order in which they are listed on the examination. You may, for example, wish to answer item number 10 before answering item number 9, etc.

Write your name on each sheet of paper used.

To be sure that each sheet you use can be correctly identified in case the examination papers are accidently mixed, write your name on each sheet of paper used for your answers.

HOW TO ANSWER THE ALTERNATE-RESPONSE ITEM

Some sample alternate-response items[1]

> *Directions:* Read each statement below. Place a plus in the parenthesis (+) before each true statement; place a minus in the parenthesis (—) before each false statement.
>
> (—) 1. It is a good policy to "cram" for an examination.
> (—) 2. A majority of the students who enter college remain long enough to graduate.
> (—) 3. If one has enough scholastic ability, success in school is assured.
> (+) 4. Learning is a process of changing one's behavior.
> (+) 5. For every hour spent in class per week, one should spend at least two hours in study.

The answers to the alternate response items above have been inserted in the answer spaces. If the answers to alternate-response items are to be placed on special answer sheets to be scored by a machine, the directions will be similar to these below, and the answers will be marked as on the sample answer sheet.

Directions: Read each statement below. If the statement is *true,* blacken the space under the "T"; if the statement is *false,* blacken the space under the "F."

6. The first step in vocabulary building is to obtain a good abridged dictionary.

7. Interpolating means going beyond the given information.

The answer to item number 6 is *true*, so the space under the T has been blackened. The answer to item number 7 is *false.* The space under the F has been blackened. Not all machine answer sheets have the same format or design; some will have question (test item) numbers running across the page, instead

---

[1] Most of the sample objective items used in this section have been taken from the materials in this book. The answers have been inserted in the answer spaces provided. Check these answers with your understanding of the materials in this book.

of as in the preceding illustration, where the test item numbers are arranged in a vertical column running from top to bottom. However, the rules and principles for marking them are the same.

Read each statement at least twice.

Be sure that you have understood the alternate-response statement. It is a good policy to read each statement twice before attempting to mark it "true" or "false." Be on the lookout for words or phrases that will make an otherwise true statement false. Although an examination item should not be designed to be "tricky," some will "throw you" unless you read them carefully. The two illustrations below show how a statement carelessly read may lead to wrong answers.

(—) Harry S. Truman, born in Independence, Missouri, was 33rd president of the United States.

(—) Henry L. Stimson was Secretary of War during World War I.

The phrase, *Independence, Missouri* in the first item, and *World War I* in the second item make otherwise true statements false. Harry S. Truman was born at Lamar, Missouri, and Henry L. Stimson was Secretary of War during World War II.

Analyze each item.

When answering alternate-response items of the "true-false" type, think along these lines: In the light of the facts and principles so far studied, would this statement be true? If you can recall proof of its truth, mark it true. If you cannot think of anything that would make it true, ask yourself "What facts and principles have I learned that would make it false?" If you can think of nothing which would either prove its truth or falsity, then *omit* that item if in the scoring a formula will be used in which the total number of your wrong answers will be subtracted from the total number of your right answers in arriving at your score. It is all right to guess if the directions indicate that such a formula will not be used in scoring your paper. In this case, guessing is encouraged if the amount of your information is such as to make your guesses better than would result from chance alone.

Look for clues.

Although well constructed test items will not contain clues, there are times when you might be able to spot a word or phrase in the item which will help you to arrive at the correct answer. For example, in true-false items the use of such broad generalizations as all, always, never, sole, etc., are likely to make all statements containing them *false*. On the otherhand, statements containing such modifiers as generally, usually, most and similar words are probably *true*.

Consider the whole statement.

Always remember that if a *part* of the true-false statement is false, the whole statement should be marked *false*.

First "hunch" is usually best.

If after marking a statement true or false, it is better not to change your answer unless you have substantial reason for doing so. Studies tend to indicate that where a student is doubtful about an answer in a true-false test, his *first hunch* is usually the correct one. These studies have shown that the student who changes his answer usually changes a correct answer to an incorrect one.

HOW TO ANSWER THE MULTIPLE-CHOICE ITEM

—Some sample multiple-choice items

Directions: For each of the statements, questions, or problem situations, below, there are five possible answers. Only one is correct or best. In each case select the correct or best answer and place the *number* of this answer in the parenthesis before each statement or question.

(1) 9. When preparing long and difficult assignments, you should

1. study immediately following the class if the schedule will allow
2. study while relaxed on a couch
3. study immediately after a full meal
4. avoid studying just before bed-time
5. arrange a study period which will last at least four hours without a break

(4) 10. Which of the following is not an effective study habit?

1. Distributing learning over several practice periods
2. Studying in the same place each day
3. Studying with the temperature of the room around 68°F.
4. Having a separate notebook for each of your classes
5. Revising classnotes immediately after class

(2) 11. An efficient student

1. studies with the radio volume lowered
2. studies at least two hours for each hour spent in class each week
3. does most of his reviewing just prior to an examination
4. does not make notations in his textbook
5. begins writing the examination as soon as the examination questions are placed in his hands

(3) 12. A man is found unconscious in a car with the windows closed and motor still running. The most important thing to do is—

1. call a doctor
2. take the man to the hospital
3. take the man out of the car
4. give artificial respiration
5. rub his arms and legs

(4) 13. Glove is to hand as shoe is to _____(?)_____

1. leather
2. laces
3. size
4. foot
5. slipper

(2) 14. Look at figures A, B, and D below. Decide which of the figures 1, 2, 3, 4, 5 belongs in space C.

(4) 15. What number follows 16 in the series where the three numbers preceding 16 or 2, 4, 8.

(1) —20, (2) —18, (3) —12, (4) —32, (5) —24

(4) 16. Select the third letter of the word which correctly completes the following statement: Chicago is located in the state of   (?)

(1) —I, (2) —A, (3) —N, (4) —L, (5) —O

If the above multiple-choice items are to be answered on a special answer sheet that is to be machine scored, the directions and answers would appear as shown below. The newer form of the IBM machine-scorable answer sheet (No. 1230) is different from that shown below. On the new form, the answer spaces (and numbers) are arranged in horizontal rows instead of in vertical columns as they are below. The instructions for marking your answers are the same—"blacken the space between the lines for each item."

Directions: Following each statement, questions, or problem situation below, there are five suggested answers. After reading each item, look at the five suggested answers and decide which one is correct or best. Blacken the space on the answer sheet corresponding to the *number* of the *correct* answer.

SAMPLE:

1. Chicago is

1—1 a country
1—2 a mountain
1—3 an island
1—4 a city
1—5 a state

	1	2	3	4	5
1	⫶	⫶	⫶	▌	⫶

	A	B	C	D	E
9	▌	⫶	⫶	⫶	⫶
10	⫶	⫶	⫶	▌	⫶
11	⫶	▌	⫶	⫶	⫶

	A	B	C	D	E
12	⫶	⫶	▌	⫶	⫶
13	⫶	⫶	⫶	▌	⫶
14	▌	⫶	⫶	⫶	⫶

Eliminate obviously incorrect answers.

A well constructed multiple-choice item will not have *obviously* incorrect answers among those suggested. They will all be plausible answers. However, in the case of items where you are doubtful about the answer, you might be able to bring to bear on the item the information you have gained from previous study of the materials. This knowledge might be sufficient to indicate that some of the suggested answers are not plausible. Eliminate such answers from further consideration. You may even cross them out. Then concentrate on the remaining suggested answers. The more of the suggested answers you are able to eliminate in this manner, the more you increase your chances of answering the item correctly.

Try to complete the statement.

If the item is in the form of an incomplete statement, try to complete the statement before you look at the suggested answers. Then see if the way you have completed the statement corresponds with any of the answers provided. If one is found. it is likely to be the correct one.

Analyze the item.

In the analogies type test item, (see item no. 13, page 135, of the sample test items) look at the first two elements, *glove* and *hand,* to see in what way they are related. You might think— "glove is worn on the hand." Then look at the third element *shoe* and find among the answers provided the fourth element. This fourth element should be related to the third element *shoes* in the same manner in which *glove* and *hand* are related. Again you might think—"shoe is worn on the foot." The word foot is found among the answers provided. It is no. 4. Place this number in the parenthesis before the item. Similar reasoning is applied to item no. 14 above. This item is known as the figure analogies type. To answer this item, you might think along these lines: "The small circle follows the large hatched circle. The fourth figure is a small square. A small square should follow a large square. (Small circle followed large circle.) This large square should be hatched. (As was the large circle) In looking at the suggested answers, you find a large hatched square. This figure is no. 2. Then place this number in the parenthesis preceding the item.

HOW TO ANSWER THE COMPLETION ITEM

—Some completion items

(*Retroactive inhibition*) 17. The forgetting caused by the interpolation of similar activities after a learning experience is known as ___?___ .

(*Extrapolating*) 18. Going beyond the information given in the data to form conclusions is known as ___?___ .

Thorough learning is important.

The completion item is one which requires the *recall* of materials previously learned. This type has no clues to help you in the process of recall. In the multiple-choice item discussed above, the answer was given among the several plausible answers. Your only task was to *recognize* this answer. The completion item, then, requires a *memorizing* type of learning. The only dependable suggestions for answering this type of item is to observe all the principles of study discussed in this book. Pay special attention to the matter of *overlearning, good notes,* and *regular reviews.*

HOW TO ANSWER THE MATCHING ITEM

—See pages 118-19 for sample matching items.

Work down one column at a time.

Start with one column and work down matching all the items of which you are *sure.* In the illustration given above on operas and composers you perhaps would work down the operas column.

Attempt "blind" recall.

First attempt to recall the appropriate word without looking at the answer column. Then look at this column to see if this word is among those in the column. In the illustration above, you would look at the title of the first opera Carmen and say to yourself "Carmen was composed by ————." If you came up with Bizet, you would *then* look at the list of composers on the right to see if the name Bizet was among them. You would then write the number of this composer (4) in the space preceding the title Carmen, etc.

Eliminate terms or words already used.

After you have worked down the list as suggested above, cross out the names or terms that you have used in your "sure" answers. (Providing the test is not one which a name or term may be used more than once in matching.) This crossing out of terms narrows the field of items you must consider on the next working down the column.

Use controlled association.

When you come to an item which you are not able to match, attempt to recall *any* and *all* facts you might have concerning this item. Through the process of association, a fact recalled might provide a clue to the answer. In the illustration above, for example, if you are not able to recall the composer of a certain opera go down the list of composers and attempt to recall the operas written by each composer.

Engage in a memorizing type of learning.

Since the matching item is one of being able to *recognize* something you have previously learned, the one sure way to do well with this type of examination is to learn *thoroughly the material before the examination.* You can do this by observing the principles of study discussed in this book.

EXERCISE X

A. Responding to Objective-Type Test Items

(Some Sample Items)

These sample items will help you become familiar with items used on teacher-made *objective* type examinations and on *standard-*

ized examinations. Provisions are made for recording your answers as in the case of a teacher-made test and also as you would on a standardized examination or one which is to be scored by machine. To indicate your answer as you would on a teacher-made test, place the letter designating the answer in the space provided. The machine answer spaces below are to be used in recording your answers as you would on a standardized examination. Use *both* methods to record your answer to each item. This procedure will help you to become familiar with the way answers are to be recorded on both types. The following example will illustrate the *two* ways in which your answers are to be recorded. Example:

(A) 1. Chicago is a
    A. city
    B. state
    C. country
    D. town
    E. village

Sample Answer Spaces

1. A   B   C   D   E

In the above example, city is the correct answer. An A has been placed in the parenthesis to record your answer as you would on a teacher-made test. In the sample answer spaces, the space beneath the A has been blackened to indicate this same answer as you would record it on a separate answer sheet.

Machine Scored Answer Spaces for Items 1 Through 25

	A B C D E	A B C D E	A B C D E	A B C D E	A B C D E
1		6	11	16	21
2		7	12	17	22
3		8	13	18	23
4		9	14	19	24
5		10	15	20	25

Directions: In the parenthesis before each question, place the *letter* designating the answer you have selected. On the separate answer sheet, blacken the space beneath the *letter* of the answer you have selected.

1. ( ) Sound is related to quiet in the same way that sunlight is to—
    A—bright, B—evaporation, C—darkness, D—cellar, E—noise

2. ( ) Select the pair of words which are related to each other in the *same* way as the pair of words in (1) below.

(1) Lamp:light

    A—school:students, B—speech:applause, C—radiator:heat, D—knowledge:life, E—typewriter:key

3. ( ) Indicate which of the following terms is correctly matched.

    A—Sun:satellite, B—Neptune:planet, C—Meteor:star, D—Moon:asteriod, E—Comet: sunspot

4. ( ) Which word below means the same as controversy.

    A—conversation, B—dispute, C—discussion, D—lawsuit, E—debate

5. ( ) A word meaning a warm regard for another.

    A—passionate, B—amorous, C—devoted, D—affectionate, E—like

6. ( ) Impotent is the same as or opposite of

    A—powerful, B—troubled, C—trivial, D—defective, E—hollow, F—explain

7. ( ) If the following words were arranged to make the *best* sentence, the last word would begin with what letter?

    acquired good be habits study can

    A—h, B—a, C—g, D—c, E—s

8. ( ) A woodland always has

    A—snow, B—trees, C—beasts, D—a forester, E—hunters

9. ( ) Iron is cheaper than silver because it is

    A—duller, B—more plentiful, C—harder, D—heavier, E—less useful

10. ( ) A father is always   ?   than his son.

    A—stronger, B—wiser, C—richer, D—taller, E—older

11. ( ) A horse always has

    A—a wagon, B—shoes, C—harness, D—tail, E—rider

12. ( ) Day and night are caused by

    A—earth revolving around the sun, B—moon revolving around the sun, C—earth rotating on its axis, D—sun revolving around the earth, E—moon rotating on its axis

One number is wrong in each of the series below (items 13, 14, and 15). What should the correct number in each case be?

13. ( ) 1 6 2 7 3 8 4 9 5 10 7 11

    A—11, B—6, C—10, D—8, E—12

14. ( ) 2 4 6 8 10 14

    A—11, B—16, C—12, D—15, E—17

15. ( ) 3 6 4 7 5 9

   A—7, B—6, C—8, D—4, E—12

What number should come next in each of the series below? (items 16 and 17)

16. ( ) 35, 28, 22, 17, 13, 10, 8

   A—12, B—21, C—9, D—7, E—15

17. ( ) 32, 16, 19, 20, 10, 13, 14

   A—9, B—7, C—25, D—14, E—10, F—12

18. ( ) One-fifth of a batch of 2000 spark plugs were defective. If one-fourth of the first 1000 were defective, what fraction of the second 1000 were defective?

   A—1/20, B—1/10, C—3/20, D—9/40, E—3/10

19. ( ) If four pencils cost 10 cents, how many can be bought for 50 cents?

   A—40, B—5, C—20, D—40, E—50

20. ( ) At 3 for 25 cents, what is the cost of 2 dozen oranges?

   A—75 cents, B—50 cents, C—$1.00, D—$2.00, E—$1.50

21. ( ) If ¾ of Mr. Adam money equals ½ of Miss Eve's money and together they have $80, how much has Mr. Adams?

   A—$40, B—$53.33, C—$30, D—$32, E—$27

22. ( ) Look at the movement of the dot in the first three figures. Where will the dot be in the fourth figure if it moves again in the same way?

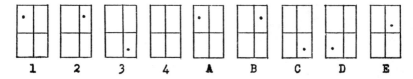

23. ( ) Look at the movement of the arrow in the first three circles. Where will the arrow be in the fourth circle if it moves again in the same way?

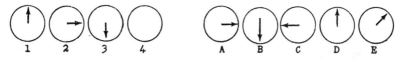

Look at drawings 1 and 2 in problems no. 24 and 25 below. If you place drawing no. 1 over drawing no. 2, what will the resulting figure look like?

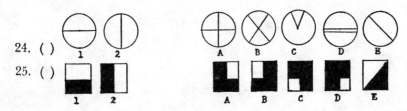

24. ( )
25. ( )

B. Essay Test Items

Make a list of the specific things you should do to improve your performance on your next essay examination.

Getting Assignments Done

There are five basic steps in attacking your reading assignments. They are as follows:

1. *Scan*—the entire reading assignment

2. *Question*—before reading

3. *Read*—to find the answers to the questions you have formulated

4. *Recite*—to see how well you have learned the answers to your questions

5. *Review*—to check on your learning, to re-learn, and to "fix" your learning

Each of these five steps is explained in detail below. Study them carefully, and put them to use in all of your reading assignments.

Scan.

Make a survey of the entire reading assignment. Do this by carefully reading the *introductory statement; summaries,* if they are provided; *main headings* (title, chapter, section, etc.); and *sub-headings* (paragraph headings, topical sentences, run-in-side headings, etc.). If you are reading an entire book, it will be important to read the *preface* and *table of contents.* Also, you will leaf through the entire book. The purpose of this scanning or survey is to get a bird's eye view of the entire book or passage. When you have some idea of what the whole is about, the parts take on added meaning. You are better able to see how "the parts hang together." Getting this bird's-eye view should not consume a great deal of time. The thing you are after in this survey is to see what the reading is all about.

Question.

As you scan or leaf through the book or passage, you will find that questions begin to come to your mind. In addition to questions which seem to come automatically, you would engage in the process of *consciously* formulating additional questions. This will result from changing headings into questions. It is important that you make a mental note of the questions which you formulate. In the beginning stages of using this method, you may even write questions in your notes or on scrap paper. The importance of remembering questions lies in the fact that your serious reading of the book or passage will be for the purpose of *finding the answers* to the questions which you have formulated. To illustrate, imagine that you are surveying or leafing through this book for the first time. From the table of contents, you notice the following headings: BUILDING ATTITUDES AND HABITS FOR STUDY AND LEARNING, ARRANGING THE STUDY ENVIRONMENT, PLANNING A SCHEDULE, etc. What are some of the questions which come to your mind? Some that could possibly result are: "What are study and learning attitudes and habits?" "How can they be developed?" "What is a study environment?" "How should it be arranged?" "How should a study schedule be planned?" In section IX, for example, a heading is Preparing for Examinations. In changing this heading into a question, you might ask yourself—"How should I prepare myself for an examination?" "What steps are involved in preparing for an examination?" As you survey or scan the materials, practice the habit of formulating many such questions from the materials.

Read.

In order to answer the questions you have formulated as a result of scanning the book or passage, some careful reading will have to be done. Before beginning this serious reading, however, *recall* the questions you formulated mentally or consult your notes if you wrote them down. Now read with an intent—an intent to *find* the answers to your questions, and to *remember* them. You will find out, after some practice with this method, that these answers seem to "stand out" from other materials. This is because you are reading with a purpose. Make a mental note of the answers you find, or make notes in your book, according to the suggestions given in section V above, to help "fix" these answers. You may also wish to make other notes in the way of cue words to help you recall these answers when you get to the next step of reciting to yourself.

Recite.

After you have read the book or passage and have found the answers to your questions, either close the book or look away from it and recite to yourself. Ask yourself the questions you formulated earlier, and then recite the answers to yourself. For example, the first sentence in this section is: "There are five basic steps in attacking your reading assignments." The question you formulated was perhaps: "What are the five steps?" Your answer to yourself might be: "The five basic steps in attacking a reading assignment are scan, question, read, recite, and review." This type of self-recitation not only helps you to check on how effectively you have learned, but it helps you to "fix" this learning. You have both *seen* the materials while reading it, and *heard* it while reciting to yourself. The more sense organs you involve in the learning process, the more effective your learning will tend to be.

Review.

If you are able to satisfactorily recall the answers during this self-recitation, then review the materials for the purpose of "overlearning" them. You will recall that overlearning reduces the chances of your forgetting the materials you learn. If you cannot recall these answers satisfactorily, then review for the purpose of relearning or learning better the materials. Taking notes while you read will prove helpful in your recall of the information.

In using the above method, *practice is important*. Without

practice, as is the case with any skill, you will not be able to get the maximum benefits from this method. One type of practice is to read materials with which you are familiar, such as newspapers and magazines. By looking at the heading in newspapers and magazines, attempt to anticipate what the passage will say. Then read the passage to check on the correctness of your guesses. This practice will increase your skill in formulating questions, and in reading to find the answers. If you expect to gain most from the method, do not omit any step. Each is important.

EXERCISE XI

The following headings appear in various sections of this book. Practice turning them into questions as suggested. Formulate at least two questions for each heading. Then check on the accuracy of your knowledge by reciting to yourself the answers to these questions you have formulated. If you are not able to answer them satisfactorily, go back and review the materials involved.

1. Building Attitudes and Habits for Study and Learning
2. Arranging the Study Environment
3. Planning a Schedule
4. Building Reading Skills
5. Developing Examination Skills
6. Building Your Vocabulary
7. Maintaining Mental and Physical Health
8. Dealing with Common Emotional Problems
9. Habits for Effective Living
10. Building Listening Skills

Maintaining Mental and Physical Health

High mental ability or scholastic aptitude in itself does not guarantee success in school work. Many persons having no more than average scholastic aptitude earn grades which are above average. On the other hand, many students with superior aptitude for school work earn only average or below average grades in school. Important factors in school success, in addition to scholastic aptitude and effective study skills, are those of *physical* and *mental health*.

You, no doubt, are already aware of the importance of physical health in any undertaking, and are able to recognize certain signs that indicate good and poor physical health. You know, for instance, that a physically fit person has good color, clear firm skin, satisfactory heart and blood conditions, good posture, etc. However, the importance of *mental health* in school work or in any undertaking is not so readily recognized by the average person. Also, at the first sign of physical illness, we usually take steps to restore our bodies to a state of good health. We consult a physician, change our diet, change the nature of our activities, or do what ever else promises to remove the illness. On the other hand, a state of poor mental health or poor adjustment may go unrecognized and untreated over a period of time, resulting in a low level of personal efficiency.

It is well established that certain of our attitudes and habits, indicative of poor mental health, can greatly impair our study and learning efficiency. The purpose of this section is to list some of the signs or symptoms which indicate the existence of conditions which, if ignored, will result in a low level of achievement or failure in school work and in other under-takings. Also, discussed in this section are the habits and atti-tudes which are conducive to good mental and physical health. Study this section carefully. Learn to recognize the signs that may mean poor mental and physical health. Take steps to formulate habits that will result in a high level of personal efficiency in school work or in any undertaking. After reading this section, take an *objective* look at your behavior. To help you examine your behavior objectively, the inventory "Effective Living"—Exercise XII—is provided. After you have answered each question *frankly,* consult the key in the appendix for the purpose of scoring and interpreting the inventory. If the results of this appraisal, or other recognizable symptoms indicate that your mental and physical health is not what it should be, take immediate steps to correct the situation. Suggestions for planning courses of action to improve your personal efficiency are given below. The final part of this section is devoted to a discussion of some practical ways of dealing with certain emotional problems which are rather common among students.

Some of the *symptoms* of poor mental and physical health are the following: (1) Inability to concentrate, (2) Insomnia (sleeplessness), (3) Chronic fatigue, (4) Underweight, (5) Excessive worry, (6) Excessive daydreaming, (7) Persistent feelings of inferiority or inadequacy, (8) Frequent periods of depression (when the future looks black), (9) Chronic indi-gestion (nervous stomach), (10) Over sensitivity (feelings easily hurt), (11) Irritability (don't get along well with others), (12) Notion that others are plotting against you.

If you have such symptoms, the first constructive step to take is to decide that you will do something about the conditions which *underlie* these symptoms. You will, perhaps, need the assistance of your school counselor in planning a course of action to resolve your difficulties. However, there is much that you can do to resolve your problems once you decide that something needs to be done. The following discussion on "Habits for Effective Living" will give you suggestions for formulating habits which will assure you of a high level of personal efficiency. The procedures for formulating personal living habits are the same for forming any habit. Review the principles of habit formation as discussed in the foregoing pages of this book.

HABITS FOR EFFECTIVE LIVING

Maintain good physical health.

Acquire hygienic habits of rest, exercise, diet, and cleanliness. A visit to a physician is a good first step to be made in the effort to improve and maintain physical health. After this first visit in which you get an over-all appraisal of the state of your physical health, follow through with periodic visits (perhaps every six months) to your physician. *Follow his suggestion for maintaining good physical health.*

Adopt and maintain an objective attitude.

An objective attitude is one in which you face your problems instead of shying away from them. An objective attitude is one in which you *attack your problems directly and rationally. You approach your problems in terms of observed facts instead of desires.* This is more easily said than done. To get some help in acquiring such an attitude, visit your counselor who will assist you in the initial stages of looking at your problems objectively.

Gain an objective insight into your own behavior.

Accept the fact that there is a *cause* for all behavior—that behavior is a means of satisfying one's inner needs. Look at *your* behavior in this light and attempt to *understand your own needs,* and to find out if they are the type that will permit a wholesome and maximum development of your potential. In other words, try to *understand why you act the way you do.* If, for example, you have shown some resentment to a classmate, ask yourself "could this act have been caused by the fact that I am jealous of this person, perhaps, because: "She has a record of superior accomplishments in school, has more boy friends, wears better clothes, etc." This does not mean that you are to constantly psychoanalyze yourself or critically analyze every behavior, but rather that you reach the place where you are able to look at your behavior more objectively. The person who can do this can be *honest with himself* and is able to *frankly admit his errors and failures*. He can accept his shortcomings and try to remedy them, or balance his shortcomings (if nothing can be done about them) by achievements in other socially approved areas. The person who can look at his behavior objectively has no need to cover up or to defend his shortcomings or failures. To gain such an insight into your own behavior, acquire all the knowledge and information you can about the psychology of adjustment. Take courses in psychology, read books in psychology, ask your teacher or counselor for a list of suggested books. You will also seek help through frequent visits to see your counselor. However, you can do much yourself to acquire self-insight by simply making an objective and deliberate attempt to understand the sources or causes of your behavior.

Develop a confidential relationship with another person.

One of the best means of reducing the tension and anxiety that tends to develop around one's personal problems is by *talking about one's difficulties*. Such is implied in the often used phrase—"talk it out" with someone. When you are able to bring your fears and anxieties into the open and talk about them they become less threatening to you. The threatening aspects of one's problems are usually the causes of irrational or unwholesome behaviors. This "talking it out" also has the advantage of bringing to bear on your problem additional information, different view points, and outside help in "sizing up" your problem. All of these factors are necessary in its solution. Talking it over with a friend also serves to give you a greater assurance—you come to see that others have similar problems, and that you are *not too different from others*. The idea that one is different from most other persons can be threatening to the individual. It can greatly impair his mental efficiency. The person who does not have another in whom he can confide usually manages to push these anxiety feelings and fears out of his conscious mind. (In technical terms, this is called repression.) These repressed feelings often come out disguised in maladjusted types of behavior. Every person needs another with whom he can talk about his intimate problems. This does not mean that you are to become wholly dependent upon this other person for the solution of your problems. You alone have the final responsibility for solving your problems. The other person can help in the solution. Neither does this mean that the other person must be a psychologist or psychiatrist. He may be a parent, husband, wife, teacher, school counselor, physician, friend.

Live in the present.

Effective living demands that we respond to the world as it *is* rather than as it *might have been*. Many behaviors, indicative of maladjustment, are caused by excessive worry about the past and undue anxiety about the future. This does not mean that we should not profit from experience, or plan for the future. However, it is essential that we deal with each situation as it arises, and in proper perspective. To view the present situation in proper perspective will demand a *relating* of the past and future. A problem or a situation cannot be viewed in terms of either the past or future as separate periods. Many non-effective responses to situations are made because the situation has been unduly colored by experiences in the past. A large number of our worries are about things over and past and can't be changed by all the worry in the world. Remember that *efficiency involves attention to the present.* Face your problems *realistically* and *attack* them *promptly* with all the resources at your command.

Develop a sense of humor.

Do not take yourself too seriously. Learn to laugh at your mistakes—admit them readily. Be able to see the ridiculous in your own conduct. This ability to laugh at your mistakes provides a safety valve against undue emotional tension. In addition, the person who can *see* and *admit* his mistakes is being objective in viewing his behavior. Objective insight into one's behavior is essential to effective living.

Assume an active attitude.

One of the essentials for effective living is that of making an *active attack* on your problems. To live effectively demands that we *do something* when confronted with a difficulty. The well adjusted person has an *active attitude*—he plans for the future, he is oriented toward a vocation, he is perfecting his work habits, etc. If one plan of attack on a problem does not bring desired results, turn to other modes of attack. The well adjusted person may daydream, but these dreams do not become substitutes of real accomplishment. The poorly adjusted student, when confronted with a problem may escape to a dream world of improbable events. His adjustment is characterized by inactivity. Assuming an active attitude does not mean mere random activity. Our responses must be selected and made after viewing the problem realistically and objectively. The responses we select in attacking a problem must be those that give promise in solving the problem. They must also be of the type that will allow us to maintain a sound state of mental health. One might respond to a problem by daydreaming. This type of response might, for the moment, serve to reduce the tension caused by the problem—the person might feel better through resorting to a world of fantasy. However, a continued use of such a response in the face of real problems will eventually lead to a state of poor adjustment. Good mental health demands that the individual *actively* respond to difficulties—not try to escape from them.

Provide for and enjoy contacts with other persons.

In our culture, effective living demands that we enjoy some human contacts. Social contacts help us in attaining an objective attitude, and in keeping active and alert in the present. In a group, each person tends to become forgetful of his own immediate needs and difficulties, while he finds satisfaction in joint achievement. Group participation tends to make anxiety and daydreaming impossible. It is through the association with others that we come to know our culture—to acquire constructive ways to deal with our problems. Effective living in a democratic culture demands that we develop skills in living with and adjusting to others.

Alternate work with rest and recreation.

Effective living must be characterized by a balance between work and relaxation. Relaxation is important to both physical and mental health. Recreational activities can aid a person to adjust more effectively. They give the individual an opportunity to "get away from it all" so that non-adjustive reactions and undesirable emotional moods may be eliminated. This temporarily getting away from the problem permits the individual to return to his tasks with renewed energy. One basic principle of learning is that time must be allowed for the forgetting of ineffective habits or responses. Rest periods and periods of recreation provide this time. Allow for rest and recreation in your study schedule and in other activities.

DEALING WITH SOME COMMON EMOTIONAL PROBLEMS

Two common symptoms of emotional problems of students are (1) *excessive worry* and (2) *feelings of inferiority or inadequacy*. Students with these symptoms are usually the low achievers or failures in school. Some suggestions for dealing with these factors follow.

A little worry or concern about your school work is not harmful—on the other hand, it might prove beneficial. As mentioned earlier, effective learning seems to require some tensions—some concern. Little learning takes place when there is no problem to be solved or when there is no *felt need* to learn. A state of complacency is not conducive to learning. *Excessive worry* is the "culprit" that reduces learning efficiency by destroying your powers of concentration. Excessive worry causes your mind to wander when attempting to study. It causes excessive daydreaming when, perhaps, you should be facing reality. Excessive worry makes it almost impossible for you to attend to what is going on in class, or to remember what you read outside of class.

In developing a course of action to reduce worry, it is best

FEELING OF
SELF CONFIDENCE...?

SUCCESS

...OR INADEQUACY?

FAILURE

to start by realizing that excessive worry is only a *symptom* of some underlying problem. When this is recognized, then it can be seen that any plan of action to eliminate worry must get at the *cause* of the worry. This is not an easy task. You will need, perhaps, the help of a counselor in the attempt to identify the sources of your worries. However, much can be done on your own. The suggestions which follow will help you to deal with excessive worry.

Attempt to see worry in proper perspective.

Many of the things one worries about *never happen,* or one frets about things over and past that can't be changed by all the worry in the world. It is estimated that only about 8 per cent of our worries are real and legitimate. If we study our worries, keeping our sense of proportion, *many of them would be eliminated.*

Talk with someone about your worries.

Talk with a counselor, teacher, parents, friends—talk with anyone. Often the act of describing a problem to another person helps you to see more clearly what is involved in your worry. In many cases, you will see that your worries are needless. Also, when you can talk about your worries (or even write about them) they tend to lose some of their disturbing qualities. As mentioned above, a thing that you can face by bringing it into the open for discussion tends to be less frightening. Fear of something (real or imagined) reveals itself through worry.

Substitute planning for worry.

It has been said that the *finest antidote to worry is work.* In order to substitute rational planning for worry, a person must formulate a plan of attack. This planning involves the gathering of information and the acquisition of new knowledge and new skills. The tendency to fear a thing (or worry about it) is lessened if one plans some attack to meet it. For example, students who have studied and reviewed their materials consistently throughout a semester or quarter will not fear (or worry about) the final examination as much as the student who has not studied and realizes at the last moment that he does not know "his stuff." The same kind of reasoning applies to all situations which tend to cause fear or worry. A person is less likely to have worries about finance if he plans a definite attack on this problem by getting a job, making a budget, controlling expenses, etc.

Related to excessive worry are *feelings of inferiority or inadequacy*. Such feelings can greatly impair learning efficiency. As in the case of excessive worry, the person with feelings of inadequacy is relieved when he is able to see himself in perspective. He can be helped to understand these feelings by talking it over with an understanding friend such as a classmate, teacher, counselor. Such a discussion often brings about the awareness that all persons have feelings of inadequacy at one time or another. When you can feel that you are not too different from other persons, the anxiety aroused by these feelings is reduced.

If an *objective* evaluation of yourself does reveal a deficiency in some area, plan a course of action to overcome the deficiency. Plan to develop other areas where you have potential if it is determined that a deficiency cannot be removed. For example, a person may shy away from social groups because he does not have *certain* social skills or ways of behaving that are characteristic of the particular group. In time he may tend to feel inferior or inadequate in all social situations. Such a person needs to plan a course of action that will result in his acquiring these social skills. Such a course of action might include the reading of books on etiquette, discussing the matter with a close friend, attending social gatherings where the proper ways of acting can be copied from persons who have already acquired the correct behaviors, etc.

Accomplishment is the best antidote for feelings of inferiority or inadequacy. There are few deficiencies that the individual cannot overcome with persistent effort. However, do not expect the impossible of yourself. Learn to accept those deficiencies about which you can do nothing. Explore and develop the talents you have in other areas. Too often, we tend to function on a level far below our potentalities. We often set impossible goals for ourselves in areas where we do not have great aptitude or potential, and neglect those areas where significant accomplishment is possible.

EXERCISE XII

EFFECTIVE LIVING

(A Self Appraisal)

Directions: Read each statement below and circle "yes" or "no" to indicate your usual behavior. Be frank in your answers. See appendix for key and interpretation of your score. Do not consult this key until you have marked each of the items with "yes" or "no."

Yes No 1. Do you worry for a long period of time whenever you are disappointed or when you fail at some undertaking?

Yes No 2. Do you often find it necessary to make acceptable excuses for your actions?

Yes No 3. Do you often find yourself blaming others for your shortcomings or failures?

Yes No 4. Do you feel that you can do most of the things you want to do without bringing on criticisms from others?

Yes No 5. Have you set definite goals for yourself? (Do you know what you want to *be* or *do* five years from now? Ten years from now? Twenty years?)

Yes No 6. Have you usually found it difficult to follow a definite plan for certain routines such as going to bed, getting up, etc.?

Yes No 7. In your conversations or discussions with others, do you feel that your point of view is *usually* the right one?

Yes No 8. Do you often find yourself worrying about the future when you are attempting to concentrate on your studies?

Yes No 9. When describing a happening to a friend, do you usually find yourself exaggerating as to what *really* happened?

Yes No 10. Is it easy for a friend to persuade you to change your **plans?**

Yes No 11. Can you do your work (school work and other) without being constantly prodded or urged by your parents, teachers, and others?

Yes No 12. Do you often feel that no one understands you?

Yes No 13. Do you usually resent being told how you should do things?

Yes No 14. Are your feelings easily hurt?

Yes No 15. Is your appetite good?

Yes No 16. Do you often feel depressed? (Does the future usually look black?)

Yes No 17. Do you make friends easily?

Yes No 18. Do you get upset easily when things don't go as planned?

Yes No 19. Have you usually been treated fairly?

Yes No 20. Are you usually suspicious of the "acts of kindness" by others?

Yes No 21. Do you often feel that people are looking at you or talking about you?

Yes No 22. Do you feel "tired and run down" most of the time?

Yes No 23. Do you usually feel disappointed with life in general?

Yes No 24. Do you tend to ridicule yourself for your shortcomings?

Yes No 25. Do you usually feel cheerful and happy?

Yes No 26. Is it always difficult for you to make up your mind?

Yes No 27. Do you often daydream about things you hope to do instead of making an honest effort to attain your goals?

Yes No 28. Do you tend to put off doing things which are difficult or which you dislike?

Yes No 29. Can you easily "forgive and forget" when you have been treated unfairly?

Yes No 30. Has studying usually been enjoyable to you?

APPENDIX

Answers to Exercises

Exercise I: Pre-test—Principles of Study and Learning
Items 5, 13, 20, 22, 24, 28, and 29 should be marked plus (+)
All other items should be marked minus (—)

Exercise VIII: A. Interpretation of Data
1-F; 2-T; 3-PF; 4-T; 5-F; 6-PT; 7-F; 8-T; 9-PF; 10-T
B. English
1-T; 2-PF; 3-T; 4-PT; 5-PF; 6-PT; 7-F; 8-PT; 9-PF; 10-T
C. Science
1-F; 2-T; 3-F; 4-PT; 5-T; 6-T; 7-T; 8-PT; 9-T
D. Mathematics
1-T; 2-T; 3-PF; 4-T; 5-T; 6-F; 7-T; 8-PF; 9-PF; 10-PT; 11-PF; 12-T; 13-T; 14-T

Exercise X: Responding to Objective-Type Test Items
1-C; 2-C; 3-B; 4-B; 5-D; 6-A; 7-B; 8-B; 9-B; 10-E; 11-D; 12-C; 13-B; 14-C; 15-C; 16-D; 17-B; 18-C; 19-C; 20-D; 21-D; 22-D; 23-C; 24-A; 25-A

Exercise XII: Effective Living—A Self Appraisal
Items 4, 5, 11, 15, 17, 19, 25; 29; and 30 should be marked *yes*
All other items should be marked *no*

Interpretation: If you have five (5) wrong answers or have marked one or more of the items 15, 17, 19, and 25 as *no*, you should plan to have conferences with your counselor for discussing ways of improving the effectiveness of your living.